The Art of Making Theatre

CONTENTS

ACKNOWLEDGEMENTS

I've read quite a lot of memoirs and began to realise that if you were born at the start of the Second World War and have gone on to live until this century, you have lived through two very different worlds. When my father came home after the war and we left Newcastle upon Tyne and moved to Birmingham, a new life began. That new life was never as clear as anything I remember from my early years during the war.

Maybe it's a privilege to have lived through these two worlds. That has helped me to become an independent person. My aim in writing this book has been an attempt to connect these two worlds. The main motivation in my life has been to connect my two interests – art and music, like my left hand and my right hand – and theatre has been the means to do so. That's how my creative life has run parallel with the art of making theatre and realizing my dreams.

I would like to thank my sister Vivien, Martin Gannon (M&B Creatives), Jane Collins, Aleš Březina, Haibo Yu, Barbara Tůmová, ROCC, Henny Dörr and all SCENOFESTees, and all my students, friends and colleagues – even if they are not mentioned in this memoir.

FOREWORD

PH about to go on a train on her own from Newcastle upon Tyne to visit her father's family in London. She had a brown luggage label tied to her coat with an instruction Change at York *and was put in charge of the guard. Approx. 1943.*

The slow cooker of memory

Memory plays a funny trick on us. In telling the story of my life, I also tell the story of making theatre. For me, the two are inseparable. All those years ago when I was a young art student in London, I was watching the customers of the renowned Cosmo Café on Finchley Road, the 'home from home' of the local émigré community. I would pass its windows daily, dreaming of how I could tell their stories. When I eventually got to realise my dream and was making the theatre piece in November 2019 as part of Insiders/Outsiders Festival, actor Frank Barrie (who played the painter Lewandowski) heard the story and said: *We have to have you in it.* It never occurred to me that I would have myself in the play as a character. I didn't want to and refused, but he said: *Well, I can't help it if you don't because you are in it.* In one sentence, Frank said what has been true all along: My life has always been part of the art of making theatre.

The dream of making theatre about the people at the Cosmo Café was not my only dream by far. I keep a storage of unrealised dreams that I record in a small notebook. That is my Arsenal of Dreams, ready to go into action, making theatre when the opportunity arises.

There is of course a great difference between memory and truth, but in the end it is memory that makes us who we are as a person – and who is to say that any of it is true or not – and, anyway, does it matter?

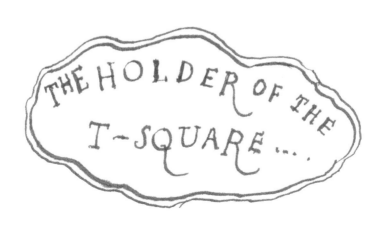

In a tiny overcrowded house in the North of England at the start of the Second World War, a young man, too young to go into the army, is dreaming of becoming an architect. He has a drawing board in one corner of a room that serves as sitting, dining and working room for an extended family. His collection of T-squares hangs from the green-painted picture rails around the room creating a dark-brown angular frieze. The room is always humming with the noise of people talking to each other in broken English, with nobody quite understanding anyone else, accompanied by the unforgettable sound of tea being sucked through sugar lumps out of a saucer. Under the drawing table, a small girl sits on a little woven-top stool watching the scene, but having an important daily job to do as holder of the T-Square for the young architect, my uncle Henry.

At the end of a day's work, provided we had not been required to rush underground into a bomb shelter, I could stand on the stool and look at what he had been drawing, and ask all the questions I wanted. At the edges of the paper, he used to draw little houses and little people seemingly in a hurry walking across squares, pushing prams or riding bicycles. Sometimes he drew crowds of people looking at something that had caught their attention, and all these people seemed to live in very big open spaces. I always wanted to know who they were, what they were doing and where they were going – and the story I was told was never enough. I later found out that these freehand drawings done in pen and ink directly onto watercolour paper were called *perspectives* and were a way in which architects were taught to visualize their ideas or dreams about buildings they might create in the future. I learned that my uncle Henry dreamed of being a painter but in those uncertain wartime days young men had to have a profession, and architecture was the nearest he could do.

In my house I have a little painting made by my uncle Henry. I discovered this small watercolour picture among the many things from my family. It shows the coast in Tynemouth in the North of England, and I find it very beautiful in its simplicity: with all the little people in it, the same that appear in his perspectives, the shadows and the sea. That work truly inspires me and what Uncle Henry drew in that watercolour painting holds true for me for any visual composition – whether it is a drawing, a sketch, a maquette or an entire scenography. They are part of the art of making theatre – the way a *scene* (*sceno-*) is *written* or drawn (*-graphy*):

> I often draw at the edges and corners of the frame, creating places where action can unexpectedly happen, very like those architectural drawings with their crowds of people at the edge of the picture that fascinated me as a child. I am attracted by the neglected, the incidental – the object that would seem to belong only to a scrapheap – the small detail that carries with it the stamp of personality and bygone use. These are powerful objects that at first glance may not seem to have anything to do with the subject, but these people and objects from the margins often become central to the scene. (*What is Scenography?* Howard 2019: xxxiii)

My mother had an older brother, Uncle Maurice, who was far away in another country during the Second World War. He was digging for water in the desert in a place called Palestine. He sent me three wooden camels linked together in a silver chain that I loved and kept by my bed. I wondered why we didn't have camels in Newcastle upon Tyne. In 1944, he sent me the most beautiful small book, full of hand-pressed flowers. The book has an olive-wood cover and hand-coloured views of Jerusalem. The titles are written in Arabic, Hebrew and English, and now, seventy-seven years later, it still looks as fresh as the day I received it. It is still my most treasured possession.

Many years later, when I fully understood its significance, I wrote:

> From the Promised Land
> In 1944, the young soldier
> Felt the smooth olive-wood book
> And saw in it pages of dried petals and branches
> Capturing the beauty of the parched land
> Where defying all conditions
> Nature survived.
>
> Each page of petals remade into a new unknown plant
> A symbol of survival
> And covered in transparent paper
> Almost too delicate to lift.

Hand-coloured between each page
A famous historic site of wonder.

Seventy-one years later the book
A little broken, but still intact
Has the inscription he wrote carefully in blue ink
For the five-year-old girl:

To Pamela, with love from Uncle Maurice, 1944.

I never forgot him:

His light has never dimmed –
He saw the beauty.

I was four years old when I started at Wingate Road Primary School. I had an aunt who was a teacher there and took me every day, always walking, for we had no car or other means of transport. The double wooden desks in our classroom were joined together by black iron rods, and two children sat side by side on seats that could not be moved. Fidgeting was not allowed. Heating in the school was minimal, and we were often cold. Small white china inkwells were sunk into a hole in the top right-hand corner of the desk (we were not allowed to be left-handed), and at the start of the day the class monitor came to each desk with a jug of black ink and filled up our inkwells, and another monitor gave out pens with steel nibs. There were no fountain pens, or biros (now called ballpoints) – though we did have them at home. Our first lesson every day was being taught to write. We had special paper with bold lines printed on it for the main body of the letter and a lower dotted line for a letter with a 'tail' and an upper dotted line for a letter with a 'loop'. Our teacher was called Miss Pilchard. (Tinned pilchards were a wartime staple food like sardines.) She was very large and very tall and wore a grey uniform. I was very frightened of her, and as I had a German surname she called me *that little German Girl* despite my aunt's remonstrations. Miss Pilchard walked up and down the aisles between the desks carrying a wooden ruler which she rapped on your hands if you made a mess. The day's writing exercise was drawn on the blackboard, which stood on an easel on the teacher's platform. We had to copy it onto our papers.

At the end of the lesson we were given a small square of blotting paper to wipe the pen nib. Our papers were collected, marked and returned the next day – and I nearly always got the full score: 10/10. I sat next to a girl called Margaret, whose mother had knitted her full-length grey wool stockings with buttons at the top that were attached to her liberty bodice. I was tremendously envious. (Liberty bodices, fleecy, lined with small rubber buttons, were part of the Dress Reform Movement, instead of corsets.) At the time, I did not know any proper English girls, and one day Margaret's mother invited me to walk across the road where we lived and to come for tea. I thanked her and said I would ask my mother and tell her the next day. When I got home from school, I was so excited to tell my mother when she came back from work. My mother worked at Floral Gowns, a dress-making workplace owned by my grandmother's brother and his wife – the only people in our family to have any money. When she came home that day, I told her the exciting news of my invitation to go for tea at Margaret's house. To my dismay, my mother and grandmother shouted in unison: *You can't go! They will give you forbidden foods!* I didn't understand what they meant. I sobbed and wept, and eventually they gave in, and a few days later I went to Margaret's house for tea. Their sitting room was calm and quiet, quite unlike our house opposite. Tea was a bowl of red jelly and a slice of brown bread, and a drink of water. They had a live black cat and a white dog, and after our tea we played with them, and then Margaret's mother crossed me over the road, and I ran home. My mother and grandmother were at the door waiting for me, and didn't ask me if I had a nice time, but immediately in unison demanded: *What did you eat?* I replied: *Jelly and a slice.* They did not know what that was, and then I said: *They have a real cat and a dog in their house*, and my grandmother hit me and said: *Don't tell lies! English people don't keep animals in their house. . . . That's just what Russian peasants do!* I cried and ran upstairs and lay on my bed sobbing – until eventually I fell asleep.

I often wonder why this event is so imprinted in my memory, for it seems so trivial and yet it was so profound. Now I realise that it was the first time I understood I was different from other children in my class. I thought that as the dreaded Miss Pilchard referred to me as *that little German Girl* on account of my surname Hoffman, and I knew there were bombs falling because we often had to sleep in underground shelters, that somehow I lived in a place called Germany. No one ever explained anything to me, and now I know this is where my lifelong pursuit of having to find out everything for myself started. And the long journey had begun . . .

My uncle Henry used to let me practise my letters after school with his used pens and nibs and black ink, and I began to love experimenting with looping letters and thick and thin marks, which in later life I have developed into my own signature style. Like many other children of my generation, and many other children throughout history, I automatically learned to understand and speak two languages and to live on both a lunar and solar calendar. As well as learning English writing, I learned to write Hebrew letters, which were cursive shapes that I much preferred, and sometimes I drew little faces in the loops. Years later, in 1954, when I started as an art student in Birmingham, we had to learn calligraphy and how to formally construct letters with compasses and rulers – first with pencil and then with pen and ink, but I found it very limiting and have never really used that knowledge. And then, after many further years, by chance – or was it chance? – I went for my first visit to Beijing, met a great Chinese calligrapher. And it was all because . . .

In 1938, a young boy aged thirteen arrived alone at Liverpool Street Station London from Berlin on the last Kindertransport that evacuated children in danger from the Nazi regime in Central Europe. (We know him now as Ralph Koltai CBE RDI, 1924–2018.) When he was eighteen, he did his National Service and was able to join his mother, who after the war had managed to get out of Germany and had a domestic job in a home in Epsom. He started going to evening classes at Epsom Art School, where he discovered graphic design and eventually registered for a full-time course, which ex-service men were able to do. This gifted and determined young man came to London, first as a theatre design student at Central School of Art, eventually to become one of Britain's most famous theatre designers working with all the national opera and drama companies. He then joined Central School of Art as a part-time teacher and, finally, as head of the Theatre Design course. A few years later I took his place. In 1997, the dean of Art suggested we should stage a retrospective of Ralph's works in our Lethaby Galleries. Ralph Koltai devised a total installation using the space in both galleries, and I was the curator. A book was published to accompany the exhibition, *Ralph Koltai: Designer for the Stage* (Backemeyer 1997). The exhibition was then bought by the British Council, which set up a tour of Southeast Asia, going to Beijing, Hong Kong, Taipei, Tokyo and Osaka.

A former Chinese mature student from my course came as our interpreter. Once the exhibition had opened in Beijing, I had some free time, and he took me on a surprise excursion. In fact, knowing of my love of free calligraphy he had set up for me a day with an aged and famous master calligrapher and painter. We went to his studio-workshop, and he began to teach me what I had always wanted to know. He had a small tree in a tub on the floor and from its branches hung all his brushes downwards so that the water could drain out of them. He then showed me how calligraphy and painting was an arm movement and not a wrist movement, like writing. He pointed out the importance of standing at the right height to allow your arm ending in the brush to flow freely over the paper in long uninterrupted lines, only thickening with the weight of the arm, and the fullness of the brush. I was so excited to practise this. As the day ended, the master presented me with the most beautiful hand-painted vertical banner made of silk on paper depicting a princess in her royal robes in blue, red, gold and white. She is carrying a golden urn of tea on a tray. Everything he taught me on that momentous day is in that banner, and when there is no sun to fade it, she hangs on the inside of my studio door. It is in fact a visual dictionary. He kept his inks and paints in china inkwells sunk into holes on his drawing table, and that image reminds me of my early days in Newcastle upon Tyne at Wingate Road Primary School.

I have always thought that exhibitions of our work should show more than one can necessarily see on stage. Theatre-making does not rest only on the action on the stage. The event can and often does include much more. As Bertolt Brecht says in his Theatre Poems, *Let the audiences see the careful preparations that have been made for them.* I have taken that as a motto in my life. By taking the production drawings and research materials out of the context of the play and assembling them together in another setting, the careful work that has gone into the preparation can be shown.

Ever since I was a child, curating exhibitions was part of our life. My uncles – my mother's two younger brothers, Henry

and Maurice, who were both architects – were members of the organization known in English as The Builders: they were the original pioneers who went to Palestine to dig the earth, plant trees and fight the desert – because trees hold water. They were part of the first kibbutz, the agricultural community in Degania in Israel, by the Sea of Galilee. But who could know about it if one didn't show it? So when they came back to England, they used to make small exhibitions that showed what they had done and the beauty of the land in particular.

My work is never complete unless there is an exhibition that comes with it. So, when I started to make theatre productions, exhibitions became a logical part of the event. One such instance is the Living Museum I made to accompany our 2017 international production of *Charlotte: A Tri-Coloured Play with Music* wherever we tour with it. (See also Chapter 8 in my *What is Scenography?*, pp. 201–30.) The exhibition contains seventy-six scale figures that we set out in scenes on the top of a piano on chests that we use on tour to move our production. To these scenes we add my drawings and the Living Museum with the contextual research, relevant information and historic facts. There spectators could come across unexpected pieces of knowledge – such as the A1 sheet about eugenics and the attempts to create a pure, Aryan race. That idea wasn't the Germans' but had already been with the Americans and before that with the British. For the Living Museum, I make such fact sheets: it's visual, but it's factual – and people are truly shocked. These are modest installations but spectators relate to them in a special way with great enjoyment. It even happened once after a show in Toronto that an elderly lady came out to find me after the performance to tell me enthusiastically: *You wouldn't believe this! There were people on stage in there and they looked just like your figures over here!*

Curating exhibitions for other people – often my artist friends – has become an indelible part of my artistic life. Just like my theatre exhibitions, in curating them I always try to show the work that goes on behind what people can see – giving them a window into the art that is often concealed. So, the exhibitions of Ralph Koltai's artwork – such as the aforementioned touring exhibition of 1997 or the more recent *Atomic Landscapes* (Cardiff 2016) – have shown a side to his creativity that audiences would never get to know coming to see his scenography for *Figaro* or *Simone Boccanegra*. And since I have known Ralph Koltai so well, I was able to shed a light on an aspect of his work as a three-dimensional artist, which I knew he always truly was, and his versatility. I knew Ralph probably like no one else, and we had a very special relationship – perhaps because I knew his story and I understood what it meant to be on a Kindertransport, growing up without his parents. Perhaps I understand him so well because he was like all my uncles put into one persona. I felt it was part of my responsibility in life to tell the story of this unique man. I also knew that in exhibitions he didn't want just pictures on the wall but an environmental installation through which people could walk and discover the artwork themselves. This is where curating exhibitions as an audience experience overlaps with the art of making theatre.

Exhibitions – like any artistic work – are never an end in themselves. The important thing is to take the first step, make a start and give the initial impulse. There is always the spin-off – the new things the impulse engenders. And unless we do something, how can any new things happen?

With all the organization that I have in my life, if I can just get to my drawing board and make a simple ink drawing, just straightaway, that's heavenly bliss.

When I draw, I am never doing it just because I want to draw a good picture; it's always telling a story, even if it's only small and ordinary people. I use my drawing to say something, to tell a story about people's lives. The two things – art and stories of people's lives – are never separate. They go hand in hand. When I was a student at the Slade, I went to lectures on the history of art by Ernst Gombrich (1909–2001). One could hardly hear him, and he spoke with a strong foreign accent, which was a familiar sound to me. What mattered most was that he linked art with stories about people. He drew our attention to various styles and introduced me to Henri Matisse's life drawings, which taught me much about the technique of the pencil. Looking at Matisse's, one can learn, for instance, that using the side of the pencil's tip one can draw volume and achieve a hundred different 'sounds' – like music. The flexibility of the pencil and the many ways it can be used depend on the variety of using one's wrist or the whole arm so that a line can also express volume. But the technique is not an end in itself. How I want to express something depends on the story I wish to tell. In that sense the way in which I draw is the same thing as the content.

The materiality of my work is very important. The surface I make a mark on is the connection between the subject and the matter. The material I work on has to excite me. Recently, I worked on *The Unicorn and Joe*, a music production inspired by the children's book *A Kid for Two Farthings* (1953) by Wolf Mankowicz (1924–98), adapted by the writer Philip Glassborow. I came across old A1 sheets of blotting paper. I made a mark on one of them, and I saw – *an adventure*. Like in music, when the composer decides on the key in which to compose the imagined sound to start the creative journey; so, the material I draw on offers that adventure of a journey to me. I love to experiment with different materials. My advice to aspiring artists is to become 'eager magpies' – as I call them – and to begin by searching for a surface to work on that feels appropriate to the text or music. Feeling is very important! Do not just use A4 copy paper – maybe card, wood, brown paper, watercolour paper, newspaper, a textile, leather – and experiment with simple mark-making until suddenly you make a mark that speaks back to you, and you are off and away.

The adventures of such a journey often bring incredible coincidences and discoveries. As I was working on *The Unicorn and Joe*, I got a call from my friend Dusty Wesker, the wife of my late friend, playwright Arnold Wesker (1932–2016). Without any background, she proceeded: *If you know someone who's very tall and can climb a ladder, there's a big portfolio for you in my garage that Arnold forgot to give you.* She said no more about it but, *There are eight of them and one of them has your name on. So you can have it.* I asked a friend who lives nearby Dusty if he could help, and he went to look at the portfolio. He told me it was absolutely extraordinary and brought it to me. The portfolio contained A1 high-quality reproductions of paintings made by the remarkable artist John Allin (1934–91).

John Allin was a character in the East End of London. As a young man he was described as a thug and regularly beat people up. He was convicted of common assault and sent to prison. It was in prison that he learned to paint, and when he was released, he met with Arnold Wesker. They found that they had memories in common – they had both grown up in the East End of London. Together they wrote a small book called *Say Goodbye: You May Never See Them Again* (1974), in which Allin painted pictures and Wesker wrote texts as if they were in conversation with each other discussing and sentimentally depicting their opposing views of their early lives in the old East End.

Allin's paintings show everyday life in East End. When Philip Glassborow came to see the portfolio alongside my drawings, he couldn't believe his eyes. This was the context of our play and John Allin had painted a Living Museum for us: *The Unicorn and Joe* is set in Petticoat Lane in the East End of London! The level of detail in John Allin's painting is fascinating, and while Allin portrays everyone, it is the people's resistance that stands out wonderfully. All the paintings show the ordinary life of all kinds of people – workers, mothers with prams, boxers and wrestlers, hairdressers, black people, white people, Jews, boys playing with hoops or at hopscotch in the street, political protests against the British Fascist movement, paper boys, men betting, neighbours in windows talking to each other, tradespeople selling toys or crying out their wares. Incidentally, the story of *The Unicorn and Joe* ends in a wrestling match, and Allin captures the world of East End wrestlers training to be boxers to earn some money.

One of the Allin paintings with Spitalfields Christ Church in the background portrays Brick Lane – where my own uncle used to live, the one I would visit as a child on the train from Newcastle to London. Another shows the beginning of Petticoat Lane with the fruit market and its fruit stalls, with people living in the entrances to the apartments. Another shows a synagogue with a fashion house on top of it, another a soup kitchen for the poor and a way in and a way out. And all the people – each captured in a moment in their ordinary lives, with unique expressions in their faces and attitudes to one another and to the happenings around them. The composition of the paintings is very dramatic, and that is true even if there is only one person in it. John Allin does not only paint places. He draws people's lives the way they lived in the East End of London at the time of his youth.

In the portfolio I got from Dusty Wesker, among the prints of John Allin's paintings, Arnold also included a special, single sheet without a painting. It is an art print of a one-page play called *The First Circle of Perception*, featuring him and his mother Leah, with Arnold giving an inventory of his life. Arnold's memory of his youth in Fashion Street became the basis for his later autobiographical play, *Annie Wobbler* (1982), for which I made the scenography. Annie Wobbler was really Arnold Wesker himself. What does this odd sheet do among Allin's paintings of the East End? What story does it tell? What discovery has the journey of *The Unicorn and Joe* taken us to?

This has to be one of the weirdest coincidences that has happened. However, this way one can meet people even when they are no longer alive, through their art. We may die but the work, and through it our story, lives on.

THE
MUSIC
DREAM

At the end of 1946, my father returned from the military hospital in Johannesburg. He had been sent there from Egypt where he had been stationed and sustained a severe spinal injury. Like so many young soldiers, he came back to a wife he hardly knew and a child he had never seen. It was not an easy reunion. I had no idea that a father was actually a man who was in your house all the time. Until then, every week, I had gone with my mother and a large bucket of water down the hill in Acanthus Avenue. There, in a garage, chocked up on wooden blocks was 'your father's car', a black Ford Prefect DOJ 379. We religiously washed and polished the car, and in my childish way I thought my father *was* the car.

One night, I was asleep in my feather bed in the little box room where all my grandparents' suitcases were piled on top of each other. It was a common practice among many émigré families never to put their suitcases away, even though they were settled in England, in case they suddenly had to move on. At about 2 am in the morning, my bedroom door opened, and two men in military uniform came into my room. I took one look and thought they were the Nazis who had come to take me away. So, I started screaming and flung myself under the bed. Of course, it was my father, who couldn't wait to see his child, and my uncle back from Palestine, who had gone to the station to meet him. My poor father was devastated. This was not what he had expected, but in those days no one thought about what was best for children as they do now. I was seven years old, and I had seen many Pathé news films of what was happening in Germany, and I was sure 'they had come for me'. And this is where my troubled life began.

These young soldiers were offered £25, a suit of clothes so they could look good for job interviews and a house where no one else wanted to live. 'Homes for Heroes', they were euphemistically called. One day, without any warning DOJ 379 arrived at our door, all my belongings were packed with me in the back, and my mother was crying as she bade goodbye to her family. And we set off – as I heard – to Perry Barr, outside Birmingham.

I remember my mother being very unhappy because she didn't know anyone there. It truly meant starting a new life: both my sisters were born there. My first sister was born in 1947 in Perry Barr, and my second sister was born in 1948 when we moved to 141 Oakwood Road, Sparkhill, in the outskirts of Birmingham. This was a typical pebble-dash semi-detached house with Tudor-style beams in the front, and a large garden at the back, facing a neighbour's orchard. The rest of our family stayed in Newcastle, so we used to drive up those 200 miles whenever we could. The journeys up north were always challenging as my father would adamantly refuse to look at the map, and the Ford Prefect DOJ 379 would always break down at the same place, just before Nottingham, near Ashby-de-la-Zouch.

One day, to my astonishment an upright piano appeared in our front garden at Oakwood Road and then was brought into the house. My father had bought it for £25 and told me I was going to learn to play the piano! A music teacher, Miss Handel in the next road, was found, and she taught me to play scales and simple nursery rhymes. She was very severe, and I didn't like her, but I loved making the sound of music.

I absolutely loved playing scales. That seemed to me a bit like the ten-times tables I learned to sing at nursery school, never realizing that they were something to do with numbers and mathematics – a subject that has been closed to me all my life. I did have two second cousins who lived on the other side of Birmingham and who were seriously working towards professional careers, one as a concert violinist and the other as a concert pianist. They took exams and played in music festivals at the City of Birmingham Literary and Music Institute – a Victorian brick building adjacent to the Town Hall and the Art College. My mother consulted them, seeking advice on a better teacher than Miss Handel, and they introduced us to the pianist and teacher Sylvia Fenby, who became the most influential person in my life. Sylvia Fenby was the daughter of the composer Eric Fenby, who was the close associate and amanuensis of the composer Frederick Delius (1862–1935) and transcribed many of his compositions for him as his health was failing. This was the musical world I had somehow fallen into, and, for me, it was inspirational and mysterious.

Sylvia showed me how many different ways to play scales there were: staccato, legato, soft and loud, making them musical compositions in themselves. She introduced me to the beauty and complexity of music as I progressed, and I began to imagine myself as a putative concert pianist dreaming of an unknown life to come. One day, she took me to the great stone building of Birmingham Town Hall, the home of the Birmingham Symphony Orchestra, to

hear a choral work called *The Messiah* by George Frederick Handel. I knew from all my family observances that we were all waiting for the Messiah to come and rescue the people of Israel from bondage, but I never guessed it would be happening in Birmingham Town Hall! The great organ pounded out, and the audience stood up for the Hallelujah chorus, and I couldn't wait to get home and tell my parents it was all going to be alright! The words *Comfort Ye, Comfort ye all ye people*, taken actually from the King James Bible, were ringing in my head.

I had just started at Kings Norton Grammar School for Girls, which turned out to be the most disastrous period of my life, but at this moment senior girls were given a new girl to 'look after', and I had Josie Levine, who was going to be a famous artist, as she told me. In the school, there were music rooms, and with her help I was able to have special times when I could go and practise my piano playing during school breaks. She was fond of the French art of silhouettes and did several of me at the piano. I began to enter for music grade examinations and quickly progressed, playing piano with the oral theory and compositional elements that were required.

Then one day, I heard that the *Prophet Elijah* was coming to the City of Birmingham Town Hall, composed by Felix Mendelssohn, a Jewish composer who had written it expressly for this venue. I determined to go, for I was familiar with the custom at family Passover gatherings of leaving a large cup of wine on the table and opening the front door during the family service in case Elijah would want to come in and join us. I went on my own to the Town Hall, bought a ticket, found my seat and heard the most beautiful and shattering music that I have never forgotten. When the soprano in a solo pleading voice sang:

Hear ye, Israel; hear what the Lord speaketh: *Oh, hadst thou heeded my commandments!* Who hath believed our report? To whom is the arm of the Lord revealed? Thus saith the Lord, the Redeemer of Israel, and His Holy One, to him oppressed by tyrants.

I vowed to myself that I would always fight against tyrants whosoever they were. I went home in a state of great excitement and told my parents not to worry because Elijah has come and was at that moment in the Town Hall, not realizing that they were sick with worry as they did not know where I had gone.

I saw in my dreams that music would be the great overrider of all conflicts and that I had to be part of it. My lessons with Sylvia Fenby continued, and she introduced me to modern composers such as Poulenc, Milhaud and especially Frank Bridge, whose piano sonata I learned to play with difficulty. I passed my Grade 8 music exam, and Sylvia then advised me before going any further, to go to a recommended physiotherapist she knew who would examine my hands and see if I would be able to sustain a career as a concert pianist. The consultation took place, and to my dismay the written report stated that my little fingers on both hands were too weak to realise my dream. I was shattered and felt my world had ended before it had even begun. I had hoped that music would elevate me into another world I did not know. Now I had to rethink and consider what other abilities I had. I remembered an earlier moment when I filled in the school questionnaire and decided not to be an airhostess or a ballerina, but to use my drawing skills to be a theatre designer, and I thought I could follow that path. I was yet to find out all the obstacles that awaited me. I gradually stopped piano lessons and began rediscovering the joy of drawing and painting, amateurish as it was. It became my ammunition for my future life.

I am fifteen, just about, at the Kings Norton Grammar School for Girls – a stone's throw from the Cadbury chocolate factory. I had always had difficulties with numbers, and I decided that I was not going to any maths lessons at all. I worked out that if I was always in the library during the maths lessons, no one would think that was untoward. Then one day, I came to school and found that my class had to go into the main hall for what they called 'a maths exam'. The examination papers were distributed on everyone's desk. I looked at it and couldn't do anything, so I decided I would draw a hotel. At one point, I became aware of a hot breath on the side of my neck. I looked up, and there was one of the invigilating teachers asking in an agitated voice: *What are you doing?!?* And I said: *I am drawing a hotel*. She pulled me by the arm up to the chief examiner at the front and said in a loud voice for everyone to hear: *This girl is drawing a hotel!* I was sent to the head mistress and was told to go home and not come back to school again. I went home and told my parents: *I am not going back to school again for a bit*, and they said: *Oh*.

About three weeks later, there was a letter for my parents which I recognized to be from the school, so I opened it, and it said that I was to go back to the school to the head mistress' room. Above the head mistress' desk were two paintings by Breughel – *Winter Wedding* and *The Tower of Babel* – and I thought: if I memorize these, I won't need to listen to anything anyone says. So, even now, I could draw both the pictures from memory, with everything in it, especially *Winter Wedding*. And thus I was expelled from school and told never to come back.

In May 1954, I walked for the last time through the iron gates of the school I hated, with joy in my heart. The fact that I had been 'expelled' was simply a release for me. Outside the school gates was a red telephone box with a paper telephone directory. I opened it, and the first page said *ART, Birmingham College of, Margaret Street, Birmingham 1* – and I resolved I would go there.

And I thought: *Oh, so that's all one has to do in life! Just go in a phone box and look it up!* So I went back home and said to my parents: *I'm not going to school anymore, I'm going to the art school*, and they just said: *Oh* – and that was that. And thus I started – but nobody helped me, nobody gave me any advice, nobody said that it would be good for me to do something – I did it entirely on my own, while everyone was telling me: You can't do this. You can't.

I grew up with one thing in my head: If you want anything, you've got to do it yourself because nobody is going to help you – not because they don't want to, but because they don't know.

Like many girls of my generation, we had a passion for collecting autographs, and we all had little autograph books with blue quilted covers that said at the beginning, *By Hook or by Crook, I'll be first in this book*, and on the back page, *Roses are red, Violets are blue. Sugar is Sweet, and So are you!* We vied with each other to see whose autographs we could get. I discovered ballet at the Birmingham Hippodrome, and after one performance I queued up at the stage door and obtained the signature of the ballerina Margot Fonteyn (1919–91). The books were sent to her dressing room for signing. I never met her. Unlike others, I also used the autograph book as a drawing book and was very proud of a triptych I had drawn in pencil. I called it *The Wilting Iris*. It showed an iris in bud, an iris rampant and, finally, an iris wilting. Then I thought, if I am going to the art school, I could take it, and I was confident that someone would like to see.

I knew where Margaret Street was as it was near the Birmingham and Midland Institute where I had gone to play the piano at music festivals. Twenty or thirty young girls had to go on the stage and play the identical movement from a prescribed piano sonata and were then given marks. A few days after I was expelled from Kings Norton Grammar School, I took myself off to the Art School. I walked up the steps into a hallway with a Victorian mosaic-tiled floor. There was no one about. I wondered what to do, until I saw a big mahogany door with gold capital letters saying, PRINCIPAL. I thought that person might be able to help me, and I walked in. There was a very large desk, with a very small old man behind it. He put a brass ear trumpet to his ear and said, *YES? – I have come to the Art School*, I said. *Would you like to see my drawing of* The Wilting Iris? – Then he said those words that have followed me all my life to this very day: *Well, you can't.* I asked him: *Why not?* – still offering my autograph book. *Because*, he said, *you have to have a grant.* Glad to have an explanation, I asked him where you get a grant from, not knowing what that was. He pointed to the City of Birmingham Education Offices across the road, and I thanked him and assured him I would be back. I walked across the road, entered a large room with benches to sit on and glass windows at one end. It was crowded, and there were long queues in front of each window. I joined a queue and finally when my turn came, the window opened and a lady shouted: *YES? – I have come for my grant*, I replied politely. *Well you can't*, she snapped. *You have to have an application form filled in by your parents. Take it home and get them to send it in* – and she slammed her window shut for I was the last in the queue and she had obviously had a long day.

I took the form home and read it through. In those days, you had to state who your grandparents were, their country of origin, if your name was the same as on your birth certificate and what your religion was. I was aware of people's reluctance to disclose this kind of information, so I filled it in myself, forged my father's signature and the next day went back to the Education Office and handed it in. A few days later, a letter came through the door of our house, in a brown envelope with City of Birmingham Education Committee stamped on the top. I opened it, and inside was something I had never seen before. I later found out it was a 'cheque'. I went immediately back to the Art College and walked straight into the principal's room, since I knew him, and said triumphantly giving him my cheque: *Here is my GRANT!* He looked at me wearily and said: *Walk down that corridor and knock on the door that says* Mr Colley *and tell him I have sent you, and he will explain to you what you will have to do.* He gave me his card, and I saw it said:

Sir Meredith Hawes. Chair. Royal Society of Watercolour Painters

I found Mr Colley's door and handed him the card and my cheque. He immediately told me I could not come to the Art School until the next year starting mid-September, and I told him I could not wait. I had to come immediately. He then asked me what I wanted to do, and conscious of the commitment I had written for the school questionnaire, I said: *Theatre Design. – Well, you can't,* he said, *but you can do embroidery.* And he showed me which door to go in. A kind lady was there, and she listened to me and explained to me about 'terms' and application forms, and asked me to make a test embroidered picture from an object in the museum and to bring it in. I still have it on my sitting room wall.

When I took it in to her, she asked me how I knew to use a sewing machine, and I told her about my mother in the war working at Floral Gowns where they had Hoffmann sewing machines, which happened to be my surname in those days, and I had learned how to use them. Then she said: *What do you really want to do?* and I told her about the theatre and the ballet and that I had read the brochure about the Art College, and it had said that Theatre Design was available. She told me that the Head of the Course was a Scotsman called Finlay James (1916–96). She said he only had two students and that they all worked with him at 'The Rep'. There and then she made a phone call and arranged for me to go and see 'Jimmy' immediately. I went and found him; he approved and said I could start straightaway. It was the beginning of the change in my life.

My parents – as was typical especially of Jewish people after the war – had one desire: to fit in and not to get noticed. There was little notion of a child behaving differently to their parents. So, it was a very unhappy and a very conflicted time for me. I am unsure if that makes one more determined in life, but I suspect it does. Music helped greatly – as it would many times later in difficult moments. I always wanted to learn music and was passionate about it. At that time, all girls of any foreign descent were sent to elocution classes to learn to talk properly, while boys went to ballroom dancing classes. If one aspired to be integrated, one also learned music. It is my greatest joy to have achieved the amount of work I have done with and through music.

My father's £25 of 'demob' (demobilization) money, which he used to buy a piano for me, started me off on another level of my life. It also meant a great deal to me as an aspiring creator. I used to see what I played in colour – and still do. The composer Aleš Březina, with whom I worked on *Charlotte: A Tri-Coloured Play with Music*, understands this perfectly, saying that sound is colour and colour is sound. When working together, he would send me a piece of music to listen to, and I would send him a picture of how it 'sounds' visually, and that was a fantastically important part of our collaboration.

My music studies went up to Grade 8 – the highest level of the British music education system – and included the basics of theory, harmony and composition. At that time, I utterly hated it, but now I am glad I did it because I can sight-read, and I can read a score and that has made a world of difference in my theatre-making. The training I had in music has helped when working with orchestras and with singers: I know when *not* to stop the music during a rehearsal, and conductors appreciate this greatly. If I were to learn it now, I would never be able to do it. At this point in my life, art and music are in perfect synchronicity. Music helps open closed doors. Music also opens the store of memories – as someone put it. We talk about memory and truth, but sometimes a simple song may remind an old person of a forgotten moment from the past. I listen to music on the radio every day – I learn from it, and it gives rhythm to my life.

When I realised that I wasn't going to be a famous pianist in my life, and I thought my life was finished at the age of sixteen, I never dreamt that music would become my partner in work because at the time we thought that there was one discipline one could be: an accountant, a teacher, an artist – but nobody thought that it was possible to be several things all at once. There was nothing like being interdisciplinary. However, one of the first things I took part in as a visual artist was an opera – still as an art student in Birmingham, going to Aldeburgh to work with the first community production of Benjamin Britten's *Noye's Fludde*.

Coming from a Jewish family, learning and knowledge is very much in the oral tradition and that from the ancient times. We have a saying: from generation to generation, it is your responsibility to pass on your knowledge and your stories. It is not up to you to make sure that people do what they are told, but you have to pass on the knowledge. I was brought up with that conviction. Sometimes people are too nervous of saying something too controversial or difficult, in case it might upset children – but there are ways of doing it. However, if one is brought up in the knowledge of this saying, the task becomes to make sure to repeat the story – to repeat it orally, and pass it on. This has become a fundamental part of what I am, and because I draw, I am also drawing stories. People often ask me about individual characters in those stories – like the characters in *The Marriage* – and want to know how come I know the characters so well. The answer is that I just drew the people in my family: I know their stories and I can draw them – and that's all I have ever done. The absolute example of that is Marc Chagall's paintings, who always painted his native Vitebsk.

When one is a child, we don't know that our roots are our roots. We learn that only through a process of discovery – by inspecting our memory we find out our identity. I was a child and I had a name – and then suddenly I was told that I had another name; of course, that meant a loss of identity. Who are you? Where do you come from? After the end of the Second World War, my father couldn't get a job because he had a German surname and like many other families he decided to change our name. One day, my father went to a phone box, opened the paper phone directory on the page starting *Ho-*, shut his eyes, put his finger randomly, opened his eyes, and it said: *Howard*. He went to the Deed Poll Office and registered for a name change. My parents had no idea what that change meant to me. They just said to me: *You're not Malka Hoffman anymore. You are Pamela Howard*. And that was it. Nowadays parents would spend hours explaining things to their children. Back then, that wasn't the case. That was probably the start of all my later troubles and the conflicts I lived through – until I regained my identity and became comfortable in my own skin, as the French saying goes. I cannot disguise the fact that I am who I am and come from where I come from – and the journey of discovery of who we are is to find how to be comfortable in our own skins, no matter where we find ourselves.

THE PARIS DREAM

In 1953, my mother answered an advert in the *Jewish Chronicle* for an English penfriend. The two mothers had somehow conversed, although neither spoke the other's language, and the first visit was arranged. I was fourteen and learned that my penfriend was called Ariane and that she lived in Paris and her father was a doctor and ran a clinic nearby. In this way, I would learn French, which was considered essential for a young lady. I was told that I would need to collect sixpences and put them into a Haig Dimple whisky bottle, and when the bottle was full, I would be able to buy a ticket to fly to Paris. We began to correspond in simple baby language – I in schoolgirl French and Ariane in more advanced English. The day came when the bottle was full. I proudly took it to the nearby bank where we lived, and when it was my turn, I politely asked the cashier for a ticket to Paris, handing her the bottle. The cashier patiently explained to me that a bank does not sell air tickets and told me where to find a 'travel agent' – and so I bought my ticket to Paris.

I had already fallen in love with ballet, having seen a few productions at the Birmingham Hippodrome, and dreamed that one day I would become a ballet designer. On my fourteenth birthday, I received a book about the Russian ballet that opened my eyes to a new world of colour, shape and movement that I determined to be part of, and then I saw that many of those artists lived in Paris. And I was going there! One of the designs in the book showed drawings by M. Georges Wakhévitch (1907–84), and I hoped that somehow I could meet him. I took my book to Paris and showed it to Ariane, and her mother, who instantly found his phone number and offered to call him and let him know that a young English girl would like to meet him. The Rozans were much grander than our family, and had a black butler who wore white gloves and served strange food like roast artichokes at the table. There were two *femmes de maison*, and Madame was in charge of La Clinique that was across the road in the Port de la Villette district. One day, the maid servant came and said, *Mademoiselle, il y a un Monsieur Wakhévitch a l'appareil* . . . and I went to the phone, and in good English he invited Ariane and me for tea that very afternoon. I had brought a small sketchbook of my drawings, and we duly appeared at his apartment. He and his wife were so generous and kind, and talked to me properly, and told me about the Ballets Russes in Paris and someone called Sergei Diaghilev, and another person called Pablo Picasso, who, he explained, was really just a painter and didn't know anything about theatre. He looked carefully at my modest sketchbook, which was mostly sketches of people I had seen, and he was the first person I ever felt took me seriously. He told me that a friend of his in London called Serge Polunin had started a course in Theatre Design at the Slade School of Art in London and that it was absolutely necessary for me to go there, and I should make that my aim in life.

I was so thrilled to have an 'aim in life' – I was walking on air! In 1956, I successfully completed the two-year Intermediate Certificate in Art at Birmingham College of Art and Design. The course didn't end with a BA Honours Degree, let alone an MA – there were no such degrees for the arts. The programme involved an examination that took two years to prepare for, and one had to pass in all the subjects if one wanted to progress to the next stage – the three-year course in the National Diploma in Design (NDD). One of the subjects of the NDD was calligraphy, which taught me how to construct a letter with a compass. At the time I hated it, but I got an exceptionally high mark for it. That taught me not just calligraphy but also resilience in creativity. I said to myself: *I hate doing this but I am going to be the best at it*. There were other skills to learn, such as perspective, object drawing, and colour and composition. To learn perspective, we had to go to Snowhill Station in Birmingham, a Victorian railway station with cast-iron pillars. We stood at one end of the platform and drew all the pillars in perspective as they receded to a vanishing point. We studied the rules of colour and composition, and learned that composing an uneven number of components in a drawing provides a firm foundation for a clear sense of focus within the structure of the work. We greeted each other in our composition classes with the phrase: *Always 3, 5 or 7; never 2, 4, 6 or 8*. After two years, I obtained my Intermediate Certificate in Art and went on to the National Diploma in Design for the stage.

The NDD allowed students to specialize in a 'craft'. The prospectus offered Theatre Design under the tutelage of Mr Finlay James, the resident set and costume designer at the old Birmingham Repertory Theatre in Station Street. He spoke with a thick Scottish accent, and when I first met him, he told me he had been torpedoed by the Japanese during the war. He then gave me a pencilled costume drawing and a watercolour paint box and asked me to paint in the colours he had marked R for red, B for blue, Y for yellow and so

on. And so, for a year I coloured in Jimmy Finlay's drawings, and I thought it was wonderful, and I was so happy! I did not realise that the Rep was not part of the Art College.

In the Rep's workshop where I did my colouring in, Jimmy had acquired a library to which I had free access. Here I discovered both the works of Edward Gordon Craig (1872–1966) and the *Studio* periodical. One issue was devoted to the Russian painter and theatre designer Léon Bakst (1866–1924), who came from Belarus, where my grandparents had come from, and M. Georges Wakhévitch, whose costume designs I greatly admired and who I thought of as 'my friend'. These were two completely different artists, both of whom were rebelling against nineteenth-century stage realism. Bakst had become part of Sergei Diaghilev's *Ballets Russes*, as had my Parisian 'friend' M. Georges Wakhévitch. I especially admired Bakst's use of the diagonal on the paper to give movement and power to the performer. Finlay James was in fact employed at the Rep as assistant to an elderly theatre designer Paul Shelving (1888–1968), who had introduced him to the works of Bakst. Shelving was incredibly generous and kind to a young aspiring girl who was clearly entranced by this new world. How strange life is, I thought, and how exciting – and I went back to my colouring in.

After some time, Jimmy Finlay returned to look at his costume designs and told me I could join the course. He did not tell me that I would be the only Theatre Design student in that year and also that the Birmingham Repertory Theatre was not the actual Art College. Apart from me there were two older girls already in the scene shop who were also Theatre Design students, and I was appointed their paint bucket cleaner.

In the scene shop at the Birmingham Rep, I met the elderly theatre designer Paul Shelving. He had come to the theatre with the theatre director and entrepreneur Sir Barry Jackson (1879–1961), the founder of 'the Rep'. Before that they both had been at the Festival Theatre Malvern, where they worked with George Bernard Shaw (1856–1950), reinventing together the stage masques and reviving the classical traditions. One bucket cleaning day, I looked in a dustbin and saw the corner of a painting. I pulled it out and saw it was a green-and-silver vision of Neptune rising from the sea, painted on a large piece of grey-green sugar paper! I immediately loved it. Then I realised Paul Shelving was looking at me. *It's a fake*, he said, but in the corner were his initials, and I asked if I could keep it. He replied grandly: *Dearest heart, take it if you want.* So, I took this painting, done in the 1930s at the time of the stage masques that Shelving realised with Shaw, and it now occupies a prominent place in my house between my windows looking on to the sea – appropriately for Neptune. Shelving was a great influence, and he spoke to me often when I was at the Birmingham Rep. We even became quite friendly. One day, he came to me with a terrible pair of pottery shoes and said: *Darling, see these shoes? – They're fakes!* He would make similar jokes and tricks. Sadly, when Shelving got old, he also became very ill – living alone and forgotten in a bedsit in Leamington Spa, surrounded by several cats. When he passed away, I was one of probably five people at his funeral. Happily his works are now in museums and archives, though many from those early Malvern days have been lost, and he has become part of theatre history.

Shelving taught me important things about pictorial composition, and these principles show clearly in his painting of Neptune. Within a large rectangle the body of Neptune with his trident strikes a strong diagonal across the paper, balanced by an opposite less powerful diagonal linking the smaller decorative elements across the paper. This composition is like a musical score but in colour and pattern, and it might serve as a basic matrix of all my visual work. *Darling girl*, he said in his typical mock-serious fashion. *If you take a piece of paper and it's portrait size, always use the diagonal! That's all you need to know.* I asked: *Is that all you need to know?* And he replied: *Certainly! If you want, you can always take another diagonal across the other way – but not so big, dear girl!* That's how Shelving taught me his main principle of composition. Now I look at his drawing of Neptune every day – and there it is: three colours, the diagonals – and the entire art of composition in one place. Paul Shelving was very formative in my work, and it was he who made me believe in myself. I asked him one day if he thought that I would ever be good enough to be a theatre designer as he was. *Dear girl, of course you can do it*, he said.

Eventually a few more embryonic Theatre Design students applied to join the course, and the Art College gave us a new space on the top floor of an old warehouse overlooking one of the canals that criss-cross the central part of the city. The practice was that the National Diploma in Design was judged on a final exhibition of each individual's work. A committee of three judges came to see the exhibits and 'interview' the students. In addition to that, there was one 'set piece' that everyone had to complete. In that year it was the Gilbert and Sullivan opera *The Gondoliers*. At 11 pm on the night before the examinations were to start, I had just finished putting up my display of exhibition boards; my father drove into town to fetch me. My interview was scheduled for the next day. At 4 am, our phone rang, and I answered it half asleep. It was the police checking if I was alive and asking if it was possible for me to come in as the warehouse was on fire. I woke my father, and we rushed up to Broad Street. Sure enough the building was in flames, and all our artwork with it. Of course, we could not go in the building, but we were all in shock. There was a mattress factory in the basement, and it appeared that someone had been smoking and left a burning cigarette butt on the floor. The next day when the fire was out, the fire rescue service lowered down from the top floor as many not completely burnt drawings as they could find. All the drawings were soaking wet and ruined as the fire service had pumped water up from the canal. We six students tried as much as we could to make light of it, but the only thing to remain relatively untouched was my scale model of *The Gondoliers*, which by a miracle I had photographed with my Kodak Brownie camera. I met with the judges some days later, and they asked me to describe my non-existent exhibition, plus the single photograph and the smoked model, and I was awarded a first-class honours degree, and, shortly after, I received the offer of a state scholarship to go to a postgraduate course of my choice. As legend goes, *Out of the Burning Fiery Furnace comes opportunity* – and remembering the prophetic words of M. Georges Wakhévitch all those years ago in Paris, I applied for admission to the Theatre Design course at the Slade School of Fine Art at University College London. I was immediately offered an interview, and my dream of going to London became a reality.

In 1959, my two years at the Slade in London arrived, and with trepidation and fear I had my first student flat at one end of Finchley Road in North West London. I was too frightened to use 'the tube' – the London Underground rail – so I used to walk every morning at 8 am all along Finchley Road to Swiss Cottage Station, where I knew I could get a bus safely to Tottenham Court Road, and then a short walk to University College. Each morning I passed the steamy windows of a café, and I used to look in and wonder who the people were in there. I noticed there were always the same

IT'S 8.30 am – WHO ARE THESE LADIES IN HATS PLAYING CARDS? I'D BETTER GO IN THE CAFE & DRAW THEM.
FIRE EXIT

group of elderly ladies, well dressed and wearing hats, and they seemed to be playing cards. I remembered what M. Wakhévitch had instructed me, which is *never* to go out without a small sketchbook in my bag and a pencil at the ready, and had impressed upon me the imperative to become 'a compulsive observer of human life'. I have always followed his advice.

One morning I was early, and on the spur of the moment I dared to go into the café. I crept into a spare seat by the door trying not to be noticed and started drawing 'The Ladies in Hats'. Suddenly I became aware that an elderly man was watching me. I looked up. *Are you drawing me?* he said in a thick foreign accent. *No*, I politely replied. *I am drawing those ladies over there. Their costumes fascinate me. – Ah, those Ladies*, he said. *They sit here all day! What else have they to do? A psychiatrist, a psychologist, a psychoanalyst, and a star from the Viennese opera. . . . It's warm and home for them here! They are glad to be alive . . . sighing and weeping for those who did not survive. . . . Playing cards, longing, dreaming of times gone by. . . . Always asking the question. . . . WHY?* I found out that this gentleman was an old Polish artist called Lewandowski, who had lived in London for thirty years. He began to tell me about all the people in the café, and I realised that this café was a kind of club. I got to know Lewandowski quite well, and we used to meet from time to time at the Polish Club in Exhibition Road and sometimes at a Polish restaurant called The Daquise in South Kensington. We always ate the same: a roast duck leg with red cabbage sauerkraut and potatoes. He was never asked what he would like or shown a menu, and I never saw him pay. He told me about his life in Montmartre and how he had 'nearly' met many of the great artists, and he gave me some good advice that reminded me of M. Wakhévitch: the importance of life drawing – as expressed beautifully in Philip Glassborow's song in *The Ballad of the Cosmo Café*:

Life Drawing – drawing from Life –
It calls on all your skill –
Drawing from life,
You come to see,
That life is never still.
Landscapes are fine,
And flowers in a vase,

Or apples in a bowl . . .
But drawing from life
When you trust your eye,
You may just catch a soul.

I wrote down Lewandowski's clear and simple words, and I thought that one day I will find a way to use them. I was familiar from an early age with the world of the émigré. I knew the language, the longings, the shoutings and the arguments from my own childhood. I knew there were always questions and never answers. I dreamt that one day, somehow, I would find a way of telling the story of this café and the world of these people but at the time I had no idea in what form.

At the Slade I found myself in the strange and mysterious world of Jean Cocteau and the Surrealists – a far cry from Birmingham. Young men walked about with pale make-up and bare feet, and some carried doves on their shoulders. It was another world altogether. Our first design project was to make some speculative drawings for Stravinsky's ballet *Apollon Musagètes*. I thought it sounded as though a mountain had to be climbed, and I found an old matchbox, and printed a construction of squares with orange, red and green paint to resemble a mountain side reaching heaven, with thin delicate tree shapes on each side. Then the day came for us six students to present our work to the two 'teachers' who were in fact well-known theatre designers from drama and ballet. I handed my painting to the great ballet designer; he looked at it briefly and threw it on the floor, saying, in a heavy accent: *Oh, Paméla. You are SO provincial!* The other famous theatre designer picked it up and looked at it for about two seconds and said to the group: *The trouble with you is you're just a middle European Jew* – and threw my painting back on the floor and left the studio. We never saw him again for at least three weeks. We were all stunned, and I thought: *I'll show them . . . just you wait and see.*

The two years passed pleasantly enough, and being in Central London gave me the chance to see exhibitions and sometimes plays if we could get free tickets. In particular, we were able to see everything at the wonderful World Theatre Seasons, where companies from all over the world brought their productions, and this is where I learned my theatre vocabulary and what I dreamt I might be able to do in the world.

By now I was getting used to navigating London, but I still walked along the Finchley Road early each morning, sometimes slipping in through the door of the Cosmo Café hoping to catch Mr Lewandowski – but sadly I discovered he was no longer in this world. However, I did come to be a semi-familiar figure and got to know one of the old ladies quite well – a psychoanalyst who lived in Swiss Cottage and was ever trying to sort out her former clients' papers in case they should come for a consultation. Sadly, she could not accept she was in another place and time. I learned that many of the customers in the café lived in a communal housing cooperative block in nearby Canfield Gardens, where they had one room, a shared bathroom and no kitchen, which is why they came to the café so early in the morning to at least get a good cup of coffee. The café was not only the *home from home* of people known as the *middle Europeans*, escaping from the troubled times in Nazi Germany, but there was also a strong Spanish element. I later discovered that the owner of the café was also a fruit importer at the old Covent Garden Market, and young boys trying to escape the Franco régime hid in the back of the lorries importing fruit from Spain to England. The enlightened owner of the café used to give them a bit of money to play music in the café – which later explained to me why the Viennese waltzes often sounded vaguely flamenco. Eventually, one of the head waiters became a world-famous guitarist!

Then in 2019, sixty years later, I had a surprise call from the art curator Monica Bohm-Duchen. She was the inspired creator of the year-long UK-wide Insiders/Outsiders Festival, and she asked me if I had anything I would like to contribute. I did not even have to search in my Arsenal of Dreams, for my ammunition was ready. I offered to create a new music theatre piece I had been dreaming about that I tentatively called *The Ballad of the Cosmo Café*. I found my sketchbook with some of the characters I had noted, hopefully unseen, all those years ago. I consulted trusted colleagues, writers, musicians and actors, and thus in November 2019 my dream of sixty years came true. Our production is now recorded on film – and a dream has become reality. The Royal Central School of Speech and Drama, located only a few steps away from the original Cosmo Café premises, offered us the use of St Peter's Church Hall in nearby Belsize Square and became our main collaborator. The Royal College of Music joined in, and I as the director/visual creator was able to assemble a wonderful cast of senior actors and singers. We set the church hall out simply with tables and chairs like the original café. At the time we had no idea how many people had memories of the Cosmo Café, but our four modest performances in an old church hall in Swiss Cottage were completely sold out, and we are still happily receiving comments and requests for a reprise.

A friend in San Diego sent this excerpt from a French television programme:

> Representing reality is never actual reality . . . you'll never agree on the details. Things happen, and that's reality, and then poof! It's over and those that lived it didn't live the same thing, don't tell it in the same way. Evidence of what happened exists but it's partial or fractured. It's impossible to repeat the entirety of the reality to those who didn't live it! (Krivine 2009)

And that's exactly what M. Wakhévitch had told me all those years ago in Paris, and why art and music can say more than words. The unique combination of music and theatre – the magic of theatre-making – can evoke memories and sentiments that reach beyond the limits of reality.

At this time, a new requirement for master's degrees was instituted in art schools. Twenty per cent of the marks had to come as a written component – an essay or a dissertation – and everybody vehemently objected, not least because many people who became artists were heavily dyslexic. David Hockney, then an MA student at the College of Art, led the protest against this motion of the Department of Education, saying that *artists did not need to write essays*. The appeal was rejected, so Hockney organized a *Not the MA Degree Ceremony*. Of course, we all went. The protest event took place on the steps outside the Royal College of Art, and there was a big table set up with some of the students sitting behind it with a scroll, ready to award the *Not the MA Degree*. Hockney came on, having dyed his hair blonde, wearing gold high-heel shoes and a gold sequin jacket. We, the audience, were his supporters cheering as he received his 'non-certificate'. That is little remembered now but it was a memorable event that meant a lot for us.

My entire house and my studio in Selsey bear positive evidence of what I call *being a war baby*. During those times, one never threw anything away. Even the government distributed posters instructing us to *Make do and mend*. There were no bins of different colours for recycling. Nowadays it's very trendy to repurpose things but that is not a new idea. Until now I never throw away a piece of cardboard, just in case I want to use it to draw on or make use of its special shape. I keep in one place all the things I use daily.

Common objects of the everyday – often disregarded or thrown away – play a big part in my creation. During the war, I learned to see the potential in ordinary things, such as chairs, tablecloths, pieces of paper, textiles and pens.

In my final years as a student at the Slade, when I got married, we met a Polish woman who lived in Notting Hill Gate in Kensington and had a spare apartment in her big house – so we were very fortunate to live in 3 Kensington Park Road, which of course we wouldn't afford today. She had a friend who lived in Paris, and when I went to Paris, I discovered the Musée Carnavalet in the Quartier le Marais. It is the Museum of the French Revolution and holds not only the famous objects but also *la quotidienne* – the objects of the everyday of revolutionary France. I was completely engrossed in them. Luckily, I had my sketchbook handy – a thing I always impress upon my students – and I drew everything, covering pages and pages of little objects, so that I could remember. Even today, looking around my house, the inspirations of the Musée Carnavalet are clearly visible. I have always been a great lover of the ordinary and the everyday – because, as the Spanish saying goes, *De pequeñas bellotas crecen los robles poderosos* (from little acorns mighty oak trees grow).

For *Rondó Adafina*, a production with the Opera Transatlántica in 2002, I needed to make a village and I wondered how I was going to do that. Then it occurred to me: it's two little chairs next to each other facing in different directions. One neighbour is sitting and one is standing, looking different ways. That's how a village was made out of two small chairs, and the image carried the atmosphere and poetics of magic realism.

When I was a child in Newcastle upon Tyne during the war, among the very few toys I had was a wooden hoop and a stick to make it roll. I used to watch other children in the street race with their hoops, but I never joined in, though once or twice I did play hopscotch with the girl across the road, who envied my American chalks. My favourite occupation in our small back garden was to make an imaginary city, putting stones and bricks inside my hoop, laid flat on the earth, always hoping that when we had to run into the shelters suddenly, my 'city' would still be there. Looking back, this may have been the foundation of my lifelong fascination with constructing stories within a round space – something I have done many times since. The world seemed to be constructed of circles – traditional dances we learned at our Sunday School classes, and especially at the nursery school I spasmodically attended when we played *Ring a Ring of Roses*, and we all fell down. Today I have plants growing in discarded industrial tyres, and they are flourishing protected by a thick circle of rubber, which I have sprayed different colours. It seems to me that a round space becomes a sacred space that encloses and unifies people who enter within its walls – like the Tabernacle, said to be built by Moses as described in the Old Testament Bible.

And my life moved on: Birmingham Repertory Theatre, March 1959. I am in the paint shop cleaning buckets for the two older students on the course. I had just turned twenty imagining this is how one begins a career as a theatre designer. The air is heavy with the smell of rabbit glue known as *size* and poisonous pigments. In between cleaning the buckets, I am cutting out canvas ivy leaves, dipping them into melted glue and, when dry, wiring them on to lengths of rope that would be draped over the gaps in the scenery where the flats depicting drawing rooms and grand houses never quite met. One day, into this mouse-ridden temple of the arts, suddenly came a young man – an actor! – and he actually spoke to us. This was extraordinary as actors never came up those black iron spiral stairs. He had momentous news. He told us that just 'down the road' in Coventry, in the new Belgrade Theatre, some writers were putting on plays about *people like us*, and furthermore, if the M1 motorway was to be finished in time, he was going to hire a car and drive the 45 miles to Coventry to see these plays, and stay overnight, or possibly even two nights. He urged us to join him, saying it was the most important event ever. We were shocked and filled with disbelief. *Don't be silly*, we said to the young Albert Finney (1936–2019), for it was he. *No one is going to write plays about people like us!* And, rather primly, we said we would have to ask our parents first. That night I related this to them, and my parents firmly warned that if I went, I would die of 'motorway madness' – and since this was the first motorway to be built, I believed them.

Notwithstanding, we three bucket cleaners and ivy-leaf makers decided to defy fate, and I was deputed to leave a polite note in the young man's pigeonhole at the stage door saying we would go. The motorway opened, and tragically just before these plays opened, the director of the Belgrade Theatre, Bryan Bailey, was indeed killed in a crash on the new motorway. The other two girls dropped out, but I was still determined to go. And so we drove those 45 miles and went to the theatre and saw the second part of the Wesker Trilogy – *Roots* (1959) – and I couldn't believe it. Not only were the plays totally different from anything I had ever seen, but they were beautiful and poetic to look at. There were no dead ivy leaves. Just a line of washing, a well-chosen chair, a perfect table and the words! Who has written this? I wondered, and who has made this beautiful staging?

There was a small café in the foyer, and we went to have a cup of tea. A tall elegant lady came up to us and said she knew we came from the Birmingham Rep. She thanked us for coming and introduced herself as Jocelyn Herbert, the designer. Jocelyn Herbert (1917–2003) said she had been in Germany and met Bertolt Brecht and that was where she had learned to *place things beautifully in the space*. Thus started a lifetime's friendship. I asked her timidly who had written these plays, and suddenly a little jovial man behind us said: *Well, actually I have – I am Arnold Wesker*, and sat down with us and asked us if we liked what we had seen. *Oh yes*, we said, and that we were staying in Coventry to see them all and something called *Look Back in Anger*. – *Well, that's not mine*, he said dismissively. Then he looked at me quizzically and said those familiar words: *Are you . . .?* and I said, *Yes* – and so I got to know Arnold Wesker and knew we would go on knowing each other.

But it was several years later, in 1965, that we met again. By this time, I was married and living in London trying to make a career for myself. Arnold Wesker had a dream – to create a new theatre space in

an old train shed in Chalk Farm Road in Camden Town, London, a venue known as the Roundhouse. The building was previously used as a wine store but had been empty and disused for some time. Its original turntable and tracks were all intact but the whole building was in disrepair. Wesker was fired by the idea of using it as a public space, open for any form of public entertainment. He envisaged theatre, dance, circus performing there and people just paying what they could afford for entrance. In 1960, the Trades Union Congress passed Resolution 42, which declared that the building should become a centre for the arts, and this gave its name to the Wesker project. From then on, it was called Centre 42. It was an ambitious and troubled undertaking from the start, but that is the nature of dreams. Dreams take an effort to realise. The ammunition needed is not just the idea but the finances to support it, otherwise it becomes like the myth of Sisyphus pushing a rock up a hill that keeps rolling down. In 1970, after ten years of effort, Wesker resigned. Our paths went in different directions – I was starting to find my way as a theatre designer, while Arnold dedicated himself to writing – but we kept in touch.

We crossed paths again when I was working in France during the 1970s. While in Paris, I saw Ariane Mnouchkine's marvellous spare production of Wesker's play *The Kitchen* (1957). The production took place in her Théâtre du Soleil in the Bois de Vincennes, adjacent to L'Arsenal, where all the records and history of French theatre are stored and which she described as *a storage for the French dream*. The way Mnouchkine produced the play – in close connection to the space – was the theatre I dreamt of making. Later at the Théâtre National Populaire (TNP) in Villeurbanne, I met the writer Michael Kustow (1939–2014), who was on an internship with the company. We talked about the popularity of the Wesker plays, and Michael told me he knew the Weskers well and that he could introduce me. And so it was that Arnold and his wife Dusty – the 'CEO of the Arnold Wesker Industry' – invited me to Bishops Road dinners – famous for food and talk and arguments. In the Weskers' house on the walls were paintings of artists they admired – Philip Sutton's Japanese prints, Lisa Dalton's paintings and John Allin's wonderful detailed paintings of Whitechapel life, especially the one of Gardiners Corner and the Cable Street Uprising, showing the clash between the British Fascist 'black shirts' and their civilian opponents. Coincidentally, the Fascists involved in the uprising were trained by Oswald Mosley in a camp of army Nissen Huts in Selsey, West Sussex – at that time known as 'Blackshirts on Sea' – where I now happen to live.

Apart from words, Arnold loved and appreciated art, and was himself a good artist. He greatly admired the linear drawings of Feliks Topolski, as I did – and this consolidated our connection. There were many readings and even rehearsals of the beginnings of his plays in Bishops Road, and later in Ashley Road, where Arnold could hear his words live, and we could gently make some suggestions.

In 1982, Arnold was writing his *One-Woman Plays* and invited me to design *Annie Wobbler,* maybe his most autobiographical play, where an old charwoman in the East End transforms into a young ambitious writer and academic. Arnold took me and the actress Nichola McAuliffe on research trips to the East End, passing places where my father's family and his own family had lived. As we walked the streets, he began telling us his memories, and this was the only time I remember Arnold talking freely about his roots. His mother's name was Leah, and their family came from Transylvania. When he was young, his parents lived in two attic rooms with the landing for a kitchen. His autobiographical play *Annie Wobbler* starts off in an attic with a kitchen on the landing, and when Annie gains some success, the play moves to a flat, and finally to a penthouse, when she becomes famous. The old flat in Fashion Street had barely changed – still the sinks and lavatories on the landings, and a rickety wooden staircase. I made numerous on-site drawings, and later four acrylic paintings, and used the details to recreate the onstage world of *Annie Wobbler*. It started at the New End Theatre in Hampstead, went on to the Fortune Theatre in the West End and won several awards. Topolski came to rehearsals and with quick line drawings captured Nichola and Arnold, resulting in the poster that was used to promote the production. I have the scale model and two of the paintings in my house and see them every day, and they remain a living memory.

All Things Tire of Themselves is the title of Arnold's only published book of poems, and the subject of many conversations we had in the last few years of his life, as his disability was progressing. Arnold was a prolific but almost unknown poet, able to sum up a whole concept of life in a few precise words. Freed from the sometimes destructive and often querulous and argumentative process of playwriting, his 'poet's pen' roamed freely through his imagination. He wrote quickly and easily without torment and with great pleasure, just saying what had to be said as if in direct speech to the unknown or known recipient. Michael Kustow summed up Wesker the poet brilliantly in his foreword to *All Things Tire of Themselves*, noting that: *silence haunts these poems, and gives them a stark honesty which touches the reader*, adding a Blakean reference that *these poems . . . harvested from three-score years and ten of innocence and experience, 'whisper in our ear'* (in Wesker 2008: 14–15). Many of the poems were written as 'gifts' to friends, and I received one after telling Arnold about my insomniac nights. It didn't solve my insomnia, but it remains a great comfort always on my bedside table. How many long nights have I tried to follow his advice from the poem!

INSOMNIA
For Pamela Howard on her 50th birthday

Tell me, reassure me.
Would I drift easy into sleep
Were passion spent?
Soft-toe myself to dream
Were nothing to disturb me
Stir me, thrill, absorb me?
Tell me. Reassure me.
If the heart, the flesh, the mind
Ceased bubbling
Would slumber sweetly come instead
And would I find my troubling calmed?
Reassure me – if the plunder came
Of all that made me
Makes and breaks me
Guides my hand, and dazzles
What imagination I was born with
Would insomnia like mist arise
And nights not sleepless be the same?

Tell me. Reassure me.
Were I to render void my being
Strip my life of what surprises and disturbs it
Could I soundly sleep again?
Drift easy into sleep again?

(Wesker 2008: 66)

Some years ago, I was a guest lecturer at the University of Texas at Austin. The curator of the Harry Ransom Research Centre invited me to view some of the archives of famous American designers, but while I was there I spotted another section marked ENGLISH PLAYWRIGHTS, and as if beckoning me away from my own subject (which Arnold liked to do), I saw several boxes marked WESKER. I asked if I could look, and was told that they had not yet been catalogued or put in order. When I lifted the lid of just one box, I saw his familiar even black handwriting of his first drafts of poems that he had carefully preserved and filed in order of date. It was the first time I realised how central the act of writing poetry was to his creative life.

Arnold's handwriting was distinctive. Black, flowing and cursive, in a precise and regular formation, as can be seen in the title piece to our *Annie Wobbler*. His ability with 'the poet's pen' manifested itself in at least thirty beautiful, elegant line drawings in black on white paper. Drawings of mundane objects made with an old-fashioned pen nib and black ink flow across the paper with an astonishing sureness of touch. He drew the interiors of his Welsh house in Hay-on-Wye – papers on his desk, china, books, flowers; reality transformed. Instinctively, his compositions compare shapes and forms, and project their own reality. An unusually large drawing of a favourite Windsor chair, its curves and spindles engraved into the paper eventually seem to have a sad and solitary personality, suspended in space. Some of the smaller ink drawings have now faded into a sepia tone, and are all the more beautiful for that.

Arnold's poem 'The need to write poetry' has a final stanza that could as well be called 'The need to make a drawing':

Images pierce hearts
Convey time's birth and death
And tell that

What lives beautifully
Speaks sadness
What is compared
Explains,
Not what described.

(Wesker 2008: 20)

After Arnold Wesker's resignation in 1970, the dream of Centre 42 came to a stop. Theatre producer and former actress Thelma Holt became artistic director of the Roundhouse in Chalk Farm Road. In 1971, she invited Ariane Mnouchkine and her Théâtre du Soleil to London. Mnouchkine brought her production of *1789* and demonstrated how that round space could be used. Instead of using a 'stage', she made small stages around the perimeter of the space. Eight hundred audience members stood in the middle of the space and became *The People of Paris*. No one explained it – it was simply obvious. To the majestic sounds of Mahler's First Symphony, the story of the first year of the French Revolution began to be told, when suddenly a large figure dressed in the costume of 1789 appeared on stilts and stopped the proceedings. He declaimed that this was only one way to tell history, but there was another: the voice of the people – and with music and song each small stage began to tell their stories. Some of the actors came into the group of spectators making sure theatrically everyone was looking in the right direction. It was a never-to-be-forgotten triumphant event, and I saw it nine times and fixed it firmly in my memory box for future use.

As a producer, Thelma Holt was an internationalist and travelled to see theatre all over the world and brought it to Britain. Wherever she worked, she created a crucible of the best productions from many countries. One year, she invited the Georgian Film Actors Studio from Tbilisi in Georgia to present their famous production of Shakespeare's *Richard III* – a show designed by Georgi Aleksi-Meskhishvili that had previously won renown at the Edinburgh Festival. King Richard was played unforgettably by Ramaz Chkhikvadze (1928–2011), dubbed as the 'Laurence Olivier of Tbilisi'. This play, depicting the Wars of the Roses showed how Shakespeare's text could become a mouthpiece of current

conflicts at the moment of the Soviet Union invading Afghanistan.
Shakespeare's war against tyranny was presented in a mixture of
styles deliberately in bad taste, the actors wearing heavy make-up-
like masks, reflecting the ugliness of a despotic regime:

> England hath long been mad and scarred herself:
> The brother blindly shed the brother's blood;
> The father rashly slaughtered his own son;
> The son, compelled, been butcher to the sire.
> All this divided York and Lancaster,
> Divided in their dire division.

(King Richard III, 5.5.23–28)

Never had I seen an audience so affected and I queued outside every
performance to get in. The atmosphere of the Roundhouse was the
true scenery of the production. Its old London brick walls, some of
them broken and peeling, were enough to give the context of the
play. The designer Richard Negri (1927–99), when we were talking
about this production, said: *The walls speak. And just remember,
when you are going into the space, look at the walls and see what
you can do with them. The building is older and wiser that we are.*
On his advice, I always look carefully at the walls of any space I
work in.

In 1977, on a 'retour' from France to London, Toby Robertson
(1928–2012), the director of Prospect Theatre company who
were resident at the Old Vic Theatre, invited me to design a
production based on the poet Christopher Logue's (1926–2011)
interpretation of Part 1 of Homer's epic poem *The Iliad*. We
went to talk to Logue in his flat in Notting Hill Gate, and he
read sections of his poem to us. It was like listening to music –
but it was about the terrible devastation of war, something we
all knew about. A prestigious group of actors had been recruited,
with Don Chapman as composer and William (Bill) Louther
(1942–88) as choreographer. I was given a free range to create
something 'poetic' but 'low budget'. Bill and I began to talk and
imagine, and I drew images not at all knowing what I was doing.
We listened to the beginning of the score which was to be played
by a current popular percussion and drumming group that Toby
Robertson thought would be a great attraction for a younger
audience. I wondered what would happen if instead of putting

the musicians in the orchestra pit below the audience, a bridge was constructed high up in the 'gods' of the Old Vic – a reversal of the hierarchy. Everyone thought this was a brilliant proposal, except the musicians, who were nervous about it. But an engineer was called in, safety promised, and so we began to compose the space. The main action was with the rows of Myrmidons, and the fight between Achilles and Patroclus. Achilles's soldiers, the Myrmidons, were trained to carry out his orders without question – hence the phrase common during the Second World War, 'one of Hitler's Myrmidons'. Actor Timothy West stood at one side of the stage as a modern-day newspaper reporter, commenting on the action. I used old blue net theatre curtains at the back of the stage to evoke the sea, from which Thetis, the Goddess of the Sea and Achilles' mother, would rise.

At this time I was frequently driving through the East End of London, to visit my elderly father in Cambridge. People say I have 'a designer's eye', meaning I never pass a skip without looking to see what I could find. Along Mile End Road there were numerous old textile warehouses, and I always drove slowly as they put materials they wanted to get rid of outside on the street. Lo and behold – waiting for me to pick up it seemed – was a *huge* pile of leather skins, stained from the wet of a leaking roof, in just the colour of sand. I stopped and negotiated with the owner, paid him some money, and he helped me to fill the back of my old Morris Minor so I could hardly see out of the back window. I called Bill Louther and said: *I have found the perfect floor. I have a car full of leather skins.* And he said: *No way! Everyone will slip and fall!* I had not thought about that. Next day I went to the theatre and got on stage before anyone else, dragging a few of the skins, and I saw Bill was right. But when I turned them over, the underneath was rough like suede. I quickly flipped them all like a collage of wild animals beaten to the floor. I waited to see the reaction of the company coming in to do a movement class – and when they did, suddenly there was no problem. I also found an old unwanted painted blue gauze in the Old Vic workshops, and we cut strips the width of the stage and stretched them out with gaps – and they became the sea. I made a watercolour painting and hardly said a word, following the dictum *Don't Talk – Show.*

The musicians' bridge was engineered and installed. They got in it and were hoisted into the mid-air of the auditorium space – and

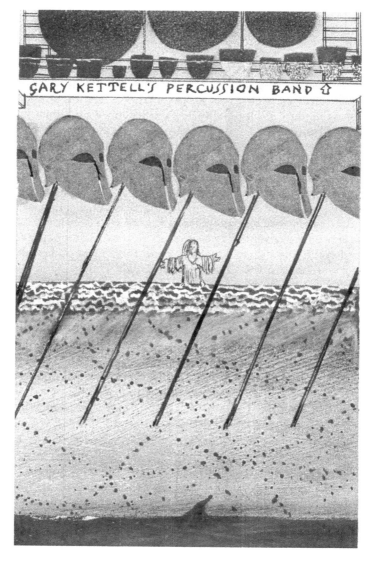

The Advance of the Myrmidons

then the trouble began. Unknown to any of us creators, an emergency board meeting had been called by the governors of the Old Vic to discuss the fact that audience members who were 'in the gods', that is, the cheapest seats, would have the best view of the musicians, while those patrons who had sponsored seats in the stalls would only see the underneath of the bridge, and that would be unacceptable. War was declared! Eventually a compromise was made, and the bridge was lowered and rehung to be at the top of the proscenium where no complaints would be likely.

The production, thirty-two years after the end of the Second World War, was immensely resonant and well received – and I realised that finding the visual metaphor for the world of the play was indeed *painting pictures with people*, just as I had learned from my days in Villeurbanne under the baton of 'the Ox from the Ardèche', Roger Planchon.

Being a practising artist and a teacher has always gone hand in hand and been complementary: I teach what I practise, and I practise what I teach. There isn't really a division between them.

This is what an initial workshop would look like. When I work, I work very closely with the text. In the process I start with the group reading around a table and then try to identify what the plot points are that move the story further on – and that's usually quite a big step, because it is not always obvious what progresses the story. So, in *Macbeth*, for instance, when Banquo takes Fleance out for a walk at night and assassins hide in a bush to kill them, but the boy runs off, there's danger – and the word *danger* can become the point of departure of one of the plot points. We need to discover these moments. Once we have found those plot points, I ask the students to draw the image of a plot point on a piece of A3 paper in about twenty minutes – without putting their own name on – and we put the drawings up on a wall in something like a storyboard. We sit in front of the display, and I ask each student in turn to tell the story just by looking at one image on the wall. Nine times out of ten the story is not what the creator has drawn, so I ask the student to take a different colour and add something in the drawing that would tell the story better. Sometimes they draw another person, sometimes a doorway or a moon. And as everybody gets accustomed to the idea that they will be interpreting someone else's drawing – which is what an audience does – they also come to reflect on their own work. We tend to think that we have done the drawing well and made our meaning perfectly clear but someone else looking at it will think differently.

That is the first introduction to the play, and I find it a very useful exercise because students come to realise that all we have to do is find the visual language that expresses the voice of the text.

The next step for the original creators of the individual drawings is to do another set of drawings that takes into account what the actual plot point is – this time adding colour and one other object. It could be a lantern, a bowl of poison, a dagger or a bush – or something metaphorical. So, in a panorama we did for Shakespeare's *Love's Labour's Lost* with students at the Hong Kong Academy of Performing Arts in 2018, we had some clouds and birds in the sky that a student suggested at one of these sessions. This phase doesn't just redo what was done previously but adds something of significance to the whole panorama.

I prefer starting simply with a figure and one object in the space rather than design the so-called set. The object becomes a kind of 'opposite' to the figure – something the figure could relate to. This relationship is the beginning of the dialogue. And then one can look at the drawing and think: What else is needed to convey the story? This is better, I believe, than making a complete scale model with a full backdrop and wings. Such task could be overwhelming at this point and unnecessary. My approach does the reverse: What is the minimum we need for the play? What does the actor need now? This is in many ways Shakespeare's trick: in *Macbeth*, he has an actor and a dagger, and then even removes the dagger and leaves only the idea of one. In other words, the two – the character and the one object – are in dialogue with one another, and that creates their world.

From there we move to the characters: Who are they? What is the world they inhabit? That is not necessarily the same thing as the first exercise. For instance, taking the character Nathaniel from *Love's Labour's Lost*, what is the world he inhabits? Who is he? What does he do in the morning when he wakes up? Does he make himself a cup of tea? What is his world? Or does he run his conjugations for his morning exercise? Shakespeare is particularly brilliant for these projects because his plays always contain opposites and that helps the characters stand out.

Another useful exercise I often use especially with Shakespeare's plays is to ask: What do characters say about themselves and what do other people in the play say about their character? I ask students to make a list that I call 'Duality in Shakespeare' and from that we can make drawings of how characters see themselves and how they appear through other people's eyes. The impressions of others often vary but reveal a great deal about the characters in the play. Often, I combine this exercise with another on costume.

I once ran a workshop in Belgrade and asked the students to think what they were going to wear the next day and what they wanted others to understand by the clothes they wore. When they came on the day, they sat in two rows opposite each other in pairs. I asked them to draw the person sitting opposite them and say what they thought the other person imagined themselves to be. Then they exchanged their images, and the confrontation was revealing: Clothes tell a story.

I never draw a costume in isolation. I start off with the gallery of characters because I have to know the people in the world of the piece. This allows me to attach stories to people and to the objects and clothes they were. In that way I can tell the actors everything about these people – what their underwear is like, or what they have for breakfast. I make a little story for each actor long before I think of the characters' environment, almost always relating them to a particular object or a material. It is the object and material that tell the story as well. So, for instance, I may tell the actor playing a character: *You've been up all night worrying about your book that you've been trying for forty years to get right, and you still haven't got it right.* And this character may be in his pyjama bottoms with a raincoat on the top. Actors relate to it, and it helps them. I always draw the character with a floor, a space and busy doing something – and every actor receives a drawing and a story.

Shakespeare's phrase from *A Midsummer Night's Dream* captures everything I create:

> imagination bodies forth
> The forms of things unknown
> and gives to airy nothing
> A local habitation and a name.

(A Midsummer Night's Dream, 5.1.14–17)

We are making something out of nothing; we are bringing from our imagination something that comes forward, and we are giving it a form, a place and a name.

Here is one such story for the character of the Lady in a Hat 2 from my 2019 London production of *The Ballad of the Cosmo Café*:

On 12 March 1938, the annexation (*Anschluss*) of Austria to Nazi Germany took place. Immediately, any person with 'non-Aryan' roots was in danger. Those who could get a visa and a train ticket got out of Vienna as quickly as possible, travelling with only a few possessions and wearing their best clothes. Often they hid their jewellery in the heel of their shoes, so the final moment before departure was a visit to the shoemaker. In *The Ballad*, Lady 2 sings that one night some soldiers came and took her husband away – *where he was going, no one would say.* . . . All she has of her former life is *the ring my true love gave to me*. Now, in 1959, she dresses every day in the few good clothes she brought from Vienna in 1938. She lives in the cooperative boarding house in Canfield Gardens – one room, shared bathroom, no kitchen. She lives in the memories of her past life at the Viennese opera. But now her actual life has shrunk to this café. Her consolation is the émigré community that has formed in 'Finchleystrasse' – the main road through North West London.

When people are suddenly fleeing to another strange country, they do their best to look as good as they possibly could. A fur coat was a status symbol. Wearing a cocktail dress at eight in the morning keeps her spirits up. Furthermore, possessing an Ascher silk scarf was an important statement, and a practical one, as it could be easily stuffed in a pocket. Zika Ascher and his family were refugees from Czechoslovakia, where they had had a thriving business. In Britain, he became 'The Prince of Prints' as the Ascher family firm, uniquely among the refugees, developed an extraordinary fashion fabric business whose calling card was the Ascher square – a silk scarf with a design from the great artists of the day. In their time, the two princesses Margaret Rose and Elizabeth were among the great customers for the Ascher headscarves and neck scarves.

Eventually, no matter what the project is, we make scale models with figures and objects and set them up in an approximate space. It is very important to be accurate with the scale and to get the proportions right. Visualizing it on the models also helps us realise that we don't need so much for the play in order to make it beautiful and *to paint pictures with people* – as Roger Planchon called it – which is the art of making theatre. In this way, making theatre scenographically becomes less 'stage design' (a notion I don't use) and more of an installation.

Edward Gordon Craig used to say to his students: *It's about time you started designing with your feet and stop designing with your eyes.* By that, he meant: *Walk the space.* To draw an analogy, he gave the example of birds marking out their territory. He devised exercises, and before his students did any visual artwork, they would walk the space. He firmly believed that one could feel the space with their feet.

I have done many panoramas with students – like the one based on Shakespeare's *Love's Labour's Lost.* In that particular workshop, I divided the play into several sections after the different situations and moments in the plot: the appearance of the women in a men's place; the women all wear newest fashion but the men are all dispossessed; the women's servants carrying their possessions, not knowing they will have to sleep in the open field; the country scenes; the palace where all the men are looking out of the window at the new arrivals. Students worked for two weeks on individual parts until an entire wall was filled with *Love's Labour's Lost: A Panorama of Life.* In this way, they created a scenographic installation from the play, retelling *Love's Labour's Lost* in physical and visual terms.

Another workshop I did was *The Metaphysical World of Macbeth* at the International Stage Art Network (iSTAN) in Beijing in China in 2017. We started with drawings inspired by Shakespeare's play and then turned the drawings into reality. We used artists' easels to create a forest of trees, the Birnam Wood; one student intuitively enlarged the drawings of figures out of all proportion, and another built a perfectly detailed tiny castle of Dunsinane out of cardboard. The result was beautiful, and it taught the students about Shakespeare, his *Macbeth* and about scenography.

Scenographic explorations such as these open the plays to theatre-making. They build closely on the dramatic text but are, at the same time, firmly rooted in a visual and material language with the actor at its centre. Theatre-making like this can bring the play to life – from the realms of dead letters and dead leaves to the power of the actor on stage to communicate with the spectator.

At the Slade School of Fine Art in 1959, we were a group of six students in the theatre studio in the basement of the building, with two 'tutors' whom we barely saw. One bonus of its location was that visitors came freely into the building to walk round the studios hoping to spot the next young British artist. In this small Theatre Design Department, we were given a speculative project – to produce some costume designs for Strindberg's *Ghost Sonata*. I was bored with making drawings and decided to do something to amuse myself. Finding some crumpled white tissue paper in a bin, I folded it into tiny pleats and carefully glued it onto a large stained piece of card rescued from another bin. So, I made a collaged figure of 'The Mummy', a character in the play. One day, a man came into the studio and introduced himself as Dick Linklater, the head of Drama at the Arts Council, and said that he had come to see emerging talent in theatre arts. Nelson Valdemar Linklater (1918–97), known to everyone as Dick or Richard, was charming and talked to each of us at length asking questions about our ambitions and hopes and dreams. I said, rather vaguely, that I hoped to be able to travel to see what people were doing in other parts of the world as well as working in London. A few days later, we were surprised to see him reappearing, and he came to me and asked if he could buy my collaged figure of the Mummy. Buy? I never knew people would buy anything of mine. He gave me a £50 note, which I had never seen in my life. I didn't even know there were such things. And I gave him my picture.

I soon discovered that the world was not waiting for me, and I started doing a series of minor assisting jobs in London. Then by chance I met Caryl Jenner (1917–73), the director of the Unicorn Theatre for Children, who were working in a derelict church hall in Wilsham Street near Shepherd's Bush in West London. She gave me the opportunity to make props and eventually to design a whole play: *The Prince, The Wolf, and the Firebird*, adapted for the theatre by Ursula Jones after a Russian folk tale – and I knew the story! I was truly inspired and did my first really free paintings, spattering imperial sheets of paper with coloured French enamel varnishes and assorted sizes of brushes until a figure was formed.

To my surprise, one day, while making some props for another production, Dick Linklater appeared. He asked me to come to his office at the Arts Council in a square just behind Piccadilly the next day at 10.30 am prompt. I had to bring my passport, which I

imagined was for entry into the Arts Council. I had no idea where
the Arts Council was but found my way, and duly his office. He
was such a gentleman and made me feel at home and welcome.
Then he told me that he wanted to ask me if I would go to Poland
for six weeks to write a report for the Arts Council on young
people's theatre. He explained that I would be given a round-trip
ticket and a plan of where to go and who to see, and everything
would be organized for me. I would however need to set off on the
following Monday. A visa and a travel plan would be prepared,
plus he gave me a paper to read that bore the title *What NOT to
do while travelling in Soviet-occupied countries*. The rest is a blank,
as the following Monday I found myself boarding a train (with a
booked seat) at Liverpool Street Station, and somehow I was in
Paris and on a train (booked seat) to Warsaw. I saw on my Arts
Council travel book that I would be met by a theatre director called
Krystyna Meissner (1933–2022), who became a great friend, and I
would stay at her apartment until the next morning when I would
board a train to Toruń, where I would go to see the new play *Tango*
by Sławomir Mrożek (1930–2013). It was a long journey and the
itinerary in my travel book very busy.

The train from Warsaw was reminiscent of a previous age. I
found my seat at the end of the carriage, and I wondered why so
many people were running up and down the carriage as if it was a
public road. They all seemed to be carrying cardboard cups. I got up
to investigate, and there between the carriages was a small rickety
shelf I had not noticed, with a very large samovar, and travellers
were bringing their own tea or instant coffee sachets and coming
to get their hot water. I knew exactly what a samovar was as my
grandparents had brought theirs with them from Minsk many years
ago. The samovar was a feature in that old kitchen of my wartime
childhood so full of their memories.

I noticed a man dressed in black with a black fedora hat
sitting across the corridor reading an English newspaper, and idly
wondered who he was. We got off the train at Toruń, and sure
enough someone was waiting for me and we went to the theatre.
Sitting next to me was an elderly man who, seeing I was clearly not
Polish, asked me in the interval: *Do you know what the national
sport of Poland is? – Football?* I replied. *Ah! No*, he said. *It's
reading between the lines.* And then he said: *Do you know what
the most expensive apartments are in Warsaw?* and in reply to me

shaking my head, he said: *It's the ones that you* cannot *see the Ministry of Culture from.* And that was my introduction to Polish ironic humour – the basis of *Tango.* At the end of the performance, my guide was waiting for me and took me to a small hotel where accommodation had been booked for the night. To my surprise, the Man in the Black Hat was already in the hotel foyer checking in. I smiled. He ignored me.

The next morning I boarded the train back to Warsaw, and Krystyna was at the station to meet me. The Man in the Black Hat was also on the train sitting opposite me. On the way to her apartment, I told her about this curious personage, and she looked at me and said: *Don't you realise he is following you – they do that here to strangers. You will see him again on the next part of your trip.* And she was proven right. *Meanwhile I am going to take you to meet a most interesting person who is the creator of Teatr Lalka, the puppet theatre for children and adults.* We walked through dark Warsaw streets that seemed to be lit by one 40-watt light bulb to a narrow street, and there behind a small front door was colour and light and I met the great visual artist and creator Adam Kilian (1923–2016). He bowed low and kissed my hand in the Polish tradition and took me into his studio. His first words to me were: *I see the world through wooden eyes.* At first I did not understand the full implication of this, but as he showed me his puppets of the fight of Saint Francis against the Devils, I immediately saw that puppets could say what humans dare not speak. I treasure the book he gave me.

During the Second World War, Adam Kilian had been stationed in Nottingham in the army, where he learned very good English. But Adam wasn't a fighter, and he used his art to say what couldn't be otherwise said. He also made supremely beautiful art full of colour at a time in Poland when nothing was available and people's lives were bleak.

I met Adam several times in subsequent years and came to know him as a true multidisciplinary artist, painting, performing, directing, making films and writing plays and poems. When he did his production of *Zwyrtala the Fiddler* in Gdańsk in 1972, he gave me the poster saying that the Fiddler at the bottom left was him and the Fiery Angel was a memory of me. It has always had pride of place in my studio. Adam Kilian's art has inspired me and others – across borders. Art does not need passports.

The next day I began the central part of my Arts Council commission – to report on Poland's provision for young people's theatre. Once again I boarded what I came to call the Samovar Express, this time crossing the country from Katowice to Gdańsk, stopping off at places en route. The Man in the Black Hat was once again sitting opposite me, this time with a copy of *The Times*. I had been given a small book *How to Say It in Polish?* with a little ink drawing on the cover of an anxious lady on a telephone and beautiful little ink drawings throughout. One of them in particular struck me: it is a drawing of a woman handcuffed and bound to a chair, and her mouth stifled by a scarf. An official with a gun in his pocket is interrogating her and is saying in Polish with phonetic English underneath: *Why don't you answer, Madam?* This book is my precious memory of that journey, which started many long friendships and other travels throughout my life, through Poland. My last but one stop was in Kraków, and I walked through a wonderful flower market in the main square in front of the National Stary Theatre. Here I saw and drew old women selling flowers from huge woven baskets, which I learned were brought daily from the Tatra Mountains above Kraków. One old lady came up to me and asked if she could see what I was drawing, and I showed her! She was delighted and mimed to me to wait while she went to fetch something – and in a few minutes she came back with a huge empty basket, asking me to accept it as a gift, which I willingly did, and using my best Polish thanked her profusely. This basket has lived in my studio ever since and is with me still. It holds my large arsenal of coloured tissue papers that I use for making scale figures and is a practical memory of that journey.

My final stop was in Wrocław, where the Arts Council had arranged for me to visit Jerzy Grotowski (1933–99) at his then embryonic Institute for Studying Acting Methods. On my detailed schedule, I was told to check in at Hotel Metropol, and somehow I found my way by following the tramlines, which I had been told always go from a station to the city centre. I went to check in at the desk, and they acknowledged the booking and directed me up the stairs to Room 26. I opened the door and to my astonishment saw six single beds. On two of the beds, men were sleeping. Returning to the reception desk, I suggested there had been some mistake, which of course they denied. I asked for a phone so I could call Krystyna in Warsaw, and she could speak to them in Polish, but they told

me: *There are no free phone lines from Wrocław to Warsaw and anyway Mr Grotowski had booked only a bed and not a room for me.* Eventually, after threatening to sleep all night in the one chair at the reception, they found a maid's room in the basement, and I spent a sleepless night there.

The next morning, I found my way to the Institute where Grotowski was rehearsing the celebrated production of Pedro Calderón de la Barca's baroque drama *The Constant Prince*. I rang the doorbell and was taken upstairs by a charming young woman who spoke good English and asked me to be very quiet. She showed me to some seats in a balcony overlooking a square performance space. Every few metres there were old-fashioned stage lamps on stands. To my surprise, *The Constant Prince*, which in my ignorance I thought was a fairy tale for children, was in fact a naked man – memorably played by Ryszard Cieślak (1937–90) – being whipped by an old-fashioned sweeping broom of twigs and screaming at the top of his voice. After three-quarters of an hour, I thought: *I have to get out of this madhouse* and started to crawl unseen, as I hoped, towards the door that I had come in. But it was in the dark, and I knocked over one of the lamps, which knocked over the next lamp, which knocked over the next lamp like dominoes, making a huge clattering noise. I ran down the stairs and opened the front door and ran as fast as I could to the hotel to collect my bag, and then to the station to get back to Warsaw. This remains in my memory of the day I did *not* meet the famous Jerzy Grotowski.

Many years later, when Krystyna Meissner was the artistic director of the Teatr Współczesny in Wrocław, she invited the Polish-English theatre director Helena Kaut-Howson to come to her theatre to direct a play, and Helena asked me to design it. We decided to offer her Howard Barker's *Victory*, which she was delighted to accept. *Victory* features very strong language, dark themes, extreme situations, and frank and rampant evocations of sex and violence. This play references the impact of the Thirty Years' War and the devastation it caused, when Poland was at the crossroads of Europe. We decided to stage this story in the traverse, by putting half the audience on the stage area and making the acting area in the centre of the whole space. This gave me the possibility of covering the floor with a waterproof oil cloth, and then putting earth over it and installing a rain bar above where water could actually fall when required. We made nettles and weeds to put in the earth, contrasting dramatically with the period costumes, showing how people try to maintain their dignity even in times of war.

I decided during rehearsals one day that I had to go out and get some fresh air. Walking through an old alleyway in the town, I suddenly recognized the front door of the Grotowski Institute that I had so shamelessly run out of. On a sudden impulse, I rang the doorbell and a very old lady opened the door. She looked at me and, in perfect English, said: *Pamela! You have come back to us! We always knew you would. . . . We never forgot you and laughed at how you made your escape. The sounds of the falling lamps and breaking glass you provided were just what the production needed, and Grotowski was very pleased indeed!*

Many years later, I returned to Warsaw and met Paweł Dobrzycki at the Academy of Fine Art. I was planning a new production of Chekhov's *The Cherry Orchard* for English Touring Theatre at the Old Vic Theatre in London. I had done several Chekhov plays, and I am a great lover of the sparseness of his words. An actor once described it to me as the equivalent of a beautiful glass chandelier, and if one crystal would be removed or put in the wrong place, the whole construction would be out of balance. Discussing this with colleagues at the Academy, Paweł suggested we go to look at Frédéric Chopin's birthplace at Żelazowa Wola not far away. It was spring, and the cherry blossoms were in full flower. When I was a young enthusiastic pianist dreaming of a future as a concert performer, my music teacher entered me into a music festival in Birmingham where the set pieces to play were a Chopin Mazurka and a Nocturne. I was very excited to have been awarded a First Prize certificate – so a visit to this shrine of the famous Romantic composer seemed more than appropriate. I was not disappointed. A small guide book was available in four languages, and inside I found the following: *When we look at the immense vase of flowers or leaves in the alcove where he was born, we have the feeling it is not a vase at all, but a fountain giving forth an inexhaustible stream of his music.* People come from all over the world to this modest cottage to drink in its beauty and refresh their spirits. There is music and concerts in the house, many great pianists come and play musical tributes to Chopin. I was shocked to find out that there were times when Chopin's music was banned in Poland and could only be heard in secret or in private salons – but history tells us that music and art cannot be suppressed. The great composer

Robert Schumann called Chopin's music *a weapon in the fight for Poland's freedom*. Chopin's music became an art in defiance of tyranny. I walked round the house with my sketchbook and found all the references I was looking for:

A large vase of lilac for the window of Anya's bedroom;
Thin gauze curtains blowing from an open window;
Window seats where people can look out into the garden of cherry trees;
Full-length windows with curved wooden tops in the ballroom looking through one room to the next;
Double windows – one opening in and one opening out to the garden;
Cherry blossom;
A curved front drive for carriages to arrive;
Falling leaves:
A leaf turned free
Is falling from the tree.

And then I was listening to Chopin's Funeral Sonata, a profound experience – and suddenly I had in my sketchbook all the images I needed for our production. Today, two small chairs and a wooden sofa I saw in the nursery at Żelazowa Wola – which Rajesh Westerberg made for our production – are in my house – filling it with stories and memories.

I went back to Kraków later independently to visit Krystyna Meissner and saw two wonderful productions by Krystian Lupa, who is both a visual artist and a theatre-maker – as I myself dreamt one day I could be. The poetic beauty of his stage creations synchronizing with the poetry of the text was perfect. During this visit, I was also able to meet another visionary, Tadeusz Kantor (1915–90), the leader of the Polish avant-garde movement, in his laboratory theatre Cricoteca. For three days, I was a welcome visitor and watched the creation of *The Dead Class*, which he later brought to Riverside Studios in London. I invited the whole company to a celebration dinner at my house, and it was a memorable event in the suburbs of southwest London! During my visit to Kraków, I was able to stay in one of the theatre's apartments for visiting artists and found these were converted from the factory where Oskar Schindler (1908–74), a member of the Nazi Party, had saved the lives of 1,200

Jews by employing them in his factory. His famous quote speaks to me: *I knew the people who worked for me. When you know people, you have to behave towards them like human beings.*

One day, having some free time I noticed a tourist bus going to Auschwitz-Birkenau and on an impulse asked the driver if I could buy a ticket. The journey took one hour and thirty minutes, and memories and stories were flooding through my brain. I walked through the entrance, under the sign *Arbeit macht frei* (labour liberates), across the railway lines and saw a group of people and heard some cheerful live accordion music: there was a bride in her wedding dress, and their family greeting their guests to this unusual venue for a celebration. I took the return bus back to Kraków, and then to Warsaw.

I had promised to make a final visit to Adam Kilian's studio before my return to England, and in his wonderful generous way he had planned to introduce me to the art of Polish paper-cutting – *wycinanki kurpiowskie* – and I fell in love with them. He took me to meet an old woman from the Kurpie district, living nearby in Warsaw, who showed me how the paper cuts were done without drawing, always by hand and cut with large sheep-shearing scissors. They were used to adorn walls and ceiling beams in small cottages in the country. Happily, instead of the custom dying out, after the Second World War an extensive initiative to develop this unique art took place, and many young girls started to learn cutting and have become true artists in paper.

Back in England, Peter Dews (1929–97), the director of the Birmingham Repertory Theatre, invited me to create a new version of Shakespeare's *As You Like It*. He wanted something 'new, innovative, unusual and colourful'. My head was full of Polish paper cuts, many of which are based on trees, flowers and birds, and I thought I could use these on a large scale, and have them made from plywood to create Shakespeare's Forest of Arden. I also proposed to incorporate cut-out flowers and birds in the same manner that could be quickly attached to the trees to indicate the changing seasons. I made a small drawing to show Peter, and he was excited about this idea. At this time, the new 'Carnaby Street vintage clothes' movement led by the Beatles was making news, and I used this resurrection of lost art in clothing for what became a famous production that transferred from Birmingham Repertory Theatre to the Vaudeville Theatre in London – in a way entirely thanks to Adam Kilian's legendary generosity for younger fellow artists.

'AS YOU LIKE IT' PROLOGUE: THE FOREST OF ARDEN
(BIRMINGHAM REPERTORY THEATRE (1966) MOBILE
TREES REFERENCING POLISH PAPERCUTS
(WYCINANKI)

In 2018, I was invited to give a keynote address in Cardiff as part of the fiftieth anniversary of the founding of the International Organisation of Scenographers, Theatre Architects and Technicians (OISTAT). I decided to make a postcard of seven important people who were part of OISTAT and have influenced my life. Each delegate who attended was given a postcard as they entered the venue. My drawing was in old-fashioned pen and ink and watercolour paint in the eighteenth-century manner of satiric cartoons. The image was also projected onto a large screen. One of the seven characters was Adam Kilian. And as I began to speak on the podium, my colleague Paweł Dobrzycki, who was sitting in the audience, sent a message to Kilian's son Jarek, who I had met when he was only aged three in Kilian's studio all those years ago. Paweł repeated to Jarek what I was saying about his father's influence on my own work. The wheel had come a full circle. As a result, now we know each other, and he has compiled a wonderful book of Kilian's interdisciplinary works which I use as a reference whenever I need to remember the joy of painting and drawing, colour and spatial composition.

Dick Linklater used a ruse to help me realise my travel dream that I told him about on that day he came into the Slade. His generosity developed into a long friendship to the end of his life. He 'collected' my work in that I used to send him drawings or small paintings especially of things related to Poland. I never actually wrote that report I was commissioned to do, and he never asked me for it. He was a true gentleman and a great director of Drama at the Arts Council. Everlasting thanks to you, Dick!

I am not a traveller, but I love being in different countries; I feel comfortable working in other languages, not worrying if I make mistakes. I never make travel plans but people invite me to different places to come and work with them – and that's how I get to know incredible places around the world. My book *What is Scenography?* has been almost like a passport. People read it and decide to invite me over. Wherever I went, I learned new things by getting to know how people live and lived – even in places where I was warned not to go anywhere on my own because it's too dangerous, like in Sao Paulo. In Salvador de Bahia in Brazil, with its history of slavery, I once did a memorable workshop called *King Macbeth of Bahia*, knowing that murders were a daily fare all around. There I saw the trapdoors where slave ships arrived; the slaves were lifted up through them as they were unable to walk after the Middle Passage across the Atlantic. Or when I was first in Hyderabad, we were served food sitting on grass in a line with the plates passed down from one to another – a beautiful custom which I thought I would use in a show one day. I haven't yet, but may still do. In this way, travelling comes back to enrich the theatre I make and my Arsenal of Dreams.

If someone were to ask me what was the greatest gift in my life, I would say it was the opportunity to travel to many different countries – not as a holidaymaker but to make work: in Israel, in Georgia, in France, in Poland, in the Czech Republic, in Serbia, in China, in South Korea, in Brazil, in Venezuela, in the United States, in Canada and in many other places. One learns to work with different people who have their own perspectives – and learn from each other. From these travels, I have made many friends and colleagues all over the world. Going out to places, creating something with people, leaving something behind and getting to know the country has in turn inspired and engendered much of my work. I could do a production of Bizet's *Carmen* in Slovenia because I had been in Spain many times and that knowledge of the country made an imprint on the opera.

Among the most remarkable travelling experiences was my visit to the West Bank in Palestine. I have been a fairly regular visitor to Tel Aviv University and Haifa University in Israel, and I always appreciated their positive integration policies – a required 30 per cent of Palestinian students in classes. The groups also included a great number of Russian émigrés and a substantial number of Turkish students. The last time I was at Tel Aviv, my group of students was very mixed, which I truly love and my hosts knew it. My hosts were Avi (Avraham) Oz and his wife, the theatre designer Tal Itzhaki. One day, they unexpectedly announced that they would like to take me for the day into Jenin in Palestine, which meant we had to cross the borderline. They took me to their car and told me: *You sit in the back and you don't say anything. The police will stop us, but we will do the answering. Do not speak, do not do anything.* In the car we came close to the barrier before Jenin's refugee camp. Suddenly, instead of going down towards the barrier, Avi turned into a field to my amazement. Behind a hedge was another car, a taxi with a Palestinian number plate. We left our car there and proceeded in the Palestinian taxi, passing through the gate, and on towards the Freedom Theatre in Jenin, where they were already expecting us. All of this had been and had to be prearranged without my knowledge. A lunch was set out, and I met all people from the Freedom Theatre, which was only just starting – among them the actor, director and activist Juliano Mer-Khamis (1958–2011). Juliano had been an actor in Hollywood. He had a Palestinian father and a Jewish mother, Arna Mer-Khamis, who had started the theatre for both performance and education purposes. The Freedom Theatre offers training in various skills from filmmaking and photography to writing and theatre-making. In the middle of our lunch in Jenin, it occurred to me what a gift I was receiving: I, a girl from Birmingham, England, am here in the West Bank in Palestine, hearing about the world.

After lunch, Juliano asked me if I wanted to see where they were constructing their new building. He also wanted to show me around Jenin to see its other sides too. He told me about the new Airbnbs that had just started to appear in the city for tourists and of the funds from the Israeli government for the construction of roads in Jenin, which the Palestinian government was misusing for other purposes. I learned more of Juliano, of his young Finnish wife Jenny, a newborn baby and twins on the way, and of his twelve-year-old daughter from a previous marriage. When he took me in his car, I naturally sat in the passenger's seat. But Juliano asked if I would mind rather sitting in the back, so I moved to the back. He showed me around Jenin, the new theatre building, as well as the new, old and bombed houses in the city. Afterwards we got back to the theatre and returned with Avi and Tali to Tel Aviv.

On the following day, Avi called me and said he had terrible news for me: Juliano was shot dead in the car where I had sat the previous day. His wife and their baby were in the car with him but were unhurt. To this day, the assassin hasn't been found. People claimed that this was the fundamentalists' retaliation for not only casting a veiled Muslim girl as the White Rabbit in a production of *Alice Through the Looking Glass*, which we also saw at the Freedom Theatre, but also for the integration of girls and boys that Juliano promoted in his theatre. A few months later, Haifa Theatre organized a memorial for Juliano. Avi sent me a ticket and without a moment of doubt, I went and flew to Israel, and heard Juliano's twelve-year-old girl make the most moving expression of what she thought of it all. I will never forget this child in a packed theatre delivering an incredible speech.

Words cannot express how much I have learned through my travels – all the escapades over the world, such as the dark days in Prague behind the Iron Curtain. I often think to myself how privileged I am to have seen both sides of many places – the official and the unofficial. I cannot claim that I have an objective or total understanding of those places, but I have been fortunate to come to great insight into people's lives.

While I don't enjoy the hassle of travel, being able to go places has been a great richness. I have been both very fortunate in this but also initiated some of the opportunities for myself – as I have always done from a very little child. My parents and grandparents knew little about English life, let alone of how people lived elsewhere. Like many émigré families, they had one concern only: keep your head down, and don't get noticed. That was the absolute mantra of my family's approach too. I am of a different ilk. While I am not saying it is better or worse, it is simply different, and it also shows the importance of travel in my life. Travel allows us a window into another culture, and all drama, music and art grow from the encounters and from the specific qualities of different countries. I believe it is the duty of art to open horizons and overcome the limitations imposed by our own cultures. Travelling makes many of these dreams possible.

.

MILESTONES

There have been moments that were true milestones in my artistic development. At those points, my life took a sudden and unexpected turn. On the spur of the moment, I would spontaneously and naively start a journey that ended up shaping my theatre-making. It was only much later that I understood the significance of those moments.

In April 1969, the annual World Theatre Season, conceived by the theatre impresario Peter Daubeny (1921–75), opened at the Aldwych Theatre London. For all emerging theatre artists, this was the essential date of the year. Everyone went to see everything, for this was our true theatrical training. The Berliner Ensemble came with productions of Bertolt Brecht's *The Caucasian Chalk Circle* and *Mother Courage*. This season also showed the work of the fabled but never seen Théâtre de la Cité from Villeurbanne, France, a company operating as a 'collective' under the direction of Roger Planchon (1931–2009). They brought *Bérénice* by Racine and *Georges Dandin* by Molière. As an embryonic theatre designer, I thought I knew the direction I would take, but when the curtain went up on René Allio's reconstruction of Dandin's world, I realised that I knew nothing about the art or craft of making theatre. Bathed in a beautiful evening light, the house, barns and outbuildings of the wealthy peasant landowner Georges Dandin were revealed. But what we saw was the entire life of the community continually moving, working and engaged in all the day-to-day jobs that had to be done. It seemed to be an animated classical French painting presented in reality. And yet it was clearly set within a theatre. Dandin's solid-built house stood at one side of the stage and the hayloft and barns at the other, emphasizing the difference between the employer and the employed. Each *personnage* came onto the stage with their own social history clearly visible. And yet this was poetry and not the prose of social realism. Each character, however incidental, acted with a force and intensity that illuminated the dilemma of George Dandin, the peasant/landowner who was 'out of his class', neither in one world nor the other. Dandin, played by the great Jean Bouise (1929–89), had to deliver several monologues directly to the audience. When Bouise did this, all the onstage world simply froze and became a still painting, which then restarted itself, as if the monologues had never happened. This simple dramatic device was not at all sentimental or picturesque. Rather, it was hard-edged, reflecting the tough endurance required to keep working on the land in hard and harsh times. This gave a clear indication of Dandin's economic standing. We saw clearly that he represented the peasant who hoped that money could elevate him into the middle classes of society. And it was clear that history is not just in the past but is living and breathing in everyday life. Quite simply, we had never seen anything like it. Could this be theatre, I wondered? If so, this was the work I wanted to make.

In 1971, I found myself, as if mysteriously propelled by some unknown force, outside the stage door of the converted swimming pool in Villeurbanne, Lyon. The Théâtre de la Cité had become the Théâtre National Populaire. I had no appointment, and I have no idea how I got there. I asked to come in, was refused and finally admitted to the *salle* where a rehearsal of Planchon's own play *La Langue au chat* was in progress. I sat quietly at the back trying to be invisible. Suddenly I realised that Planchon was standing next to me. *If you are going to be here*, he said to me in French, *you must be part of the company, not a spectator at the back*. I moved down to join the others, and thus began my next ten years as a *stagière* (trainee) and finally an *assistante à la mise-en-scène* (internee stage director). I found myself sitting next to Jean Bouise's wife, the actress Isabelle Sadoyan (1928–2017). I was clutching my small suitcase, and she asked me if I had somewhere to stay. I had quite forgotten to arrange anything, and she insisted I came to stay with them until I found a small hotel, and that she would help me. She explained that the company all ate together in the small restaurant opposite the theatre and that there might be a room there.

Sitting with the group I realised that it wasn't just the actors in the rehearsal, but it was also the technicians, the transport drivers, the kitchen staff – in other words, it was open to anyone in the company who wanted to come. At the end of the rehearsal, there was a 'comments session' where anyone could make suggestions for improvements. Where it was a technical issue, the workshops were expected to have made the agreed change by the next day.

The speed was fast, and I quickly learned from Planchon himself that the objective was to *paint pictures with people*. What did that mean? I had heard of actors entering and exiting, but this was totally different. It was like watching a film, frame by frame. Planchon would shake his head and say: *Mais non! Ce n'est pas beau!* (No! That's not beautiful!) – and the scene would start again. Fatigued as

I was from my long journey, it was totally exhilarating. I thought I was in heaven.

This was truly my awakening, and what I learned over the following ten years – *aller et retour* (going over and over), thankfully supported by the Arts Council – has stayed with me and been the foundation of all my work. During these years, I was introduced to the vibrant community of European theatre creators who knew each other and came to see each other's work. In this way, I was fortunate to meet Ariane Mnouchkine, artistic director of the Théâtre du Soleil in Paris, Giorgio Strehler from the Teatro Piccolo in Milan and Yuri Lyubimov from the Taganka Theatre in Moscow, among others. I also learned that the focus of much of their thinking was Bertolt Brecht at the Berliner Ensemble in East Berlin. As Roger Planchon used to say, *Brecht, il est bien fort* (Brecht, he is really somebody) – and I dreamt that one day I would get there too.

In 1974, at the Roundhouse in London, Ariane Mnouchkine had brought her company Théâtre du Soleil in Paris to present their performance of *1789*. After meeting her in France, and discovering that she was educated at Oxford University and that we had several friends in common, she always welcomed me to her 'home', which was her theatre. I went many times to the Bois de Vincennes outside Paris to see productions by Mnouchkine and her company, and got to know the painter/scenographer Guy-Claude François (1940–2014), and saw his method of working so closely with Mnouchkine, not just 'doing what the Director wanted' but contributing his spatial visions of the whole production. It was thrilling to see the power of the collective, the 'home' that was built, especially when Ariane came out at the start of each production and asked us to greet and shake hands with our audience neighbour, and anyone who had a car to go back into Paris should offer a lift to anyone needing it – as all transport would have stopped before the end of the performance. It worked every time, and the audience were united in warmth before anything had even begun. I was amazed that Ariane was interested in my dreams, hopes and ambitions, and she was a good listener. She gave me the best advice, which I have followed in my productions to this day, explaining: *My theatre is my house. The audience are my paying guests. From the moment they step over the threshold, they must enter a different world.* She would make an exhibition on the walls of the foyer of the context of the production

the audience would see – I call it a Living Museum. She often had a different menu in her café to correspond to the production – and, of course, the audience passed through the auditorium built on scaffolding and underneath they saw the actors putting on their costumes and make-up – all part of the event.

My great fortune was to be at the Théâtre National Populaire during the 1970s when Planchon was writing all his own plays. He did not like to travel, so when he finally agreed that one of his plays, *The Life and Crimes of Gilles de Rais: A Liturgy of Evil*, could be done by CSC, a small theatre in Greenwich Village, New York, I was dispatched to create the scenic elements. When I arrived in New York from France in snowy November, I expected that the basic elements we had requested would be ready for installation. The elements to be installed were simple – a painted floor and a ceiling of tree branches. But I was dismayed to discover that absolutely nothing had been done. I was very conscious that I was there representing the TNP. Unknown to the theatre, provisional preparations were being made for the possibility of Planchon actually coming. I also had the responsibility of being the simultaneous translator. I found a phone box and called my old and dear friends, the great American designer Ming Cho Lee (1930–2020) and his wife Betsy, and told them my sad story. Within twenty minutes they were at the corner of the street. They picked me up in their car and drove me to Central Park, where trees were being cut down, and we filled the car with branches and took them to CSC Theatre. Ming then demonstrated in no uncertain terms how to fix them to the overhead scaffolding lighting bars, and how to put an oil cloth that *he just happened to have in the back of his car* on the stage floor that could be scrunched up and scattered with dead leaves to look like a muddy field. He saved the day, and I was and am eternally grateful to him.

After this experience in New York, Planchon gave permission for the newly rebuilt Birmingham Repertory Theatre to stage his own version of the French Revolution, *Blues, Whites and Reds*. This is the first and only production of his work ever to be seen in Britain. Inspired by the work of Peter Schumann of Bread and Puppet Theatre in Vermont, with new music composed by Carl Davis, in a translation by John Burgess, who was at the TNP on a Churchill Fellowship, and directed by Michael Simpson, the production was both sensational and 'ahead of its time'. To the amazement of the actors and myself as simultaneous translator, Planchon actually came to Birmingham with his wife, the actress Colette Dompietrini (1934–2000), and his two sons.

On 12 May 2009, Roger Planchon, that indestructible Ox from the Ardèche, died suddenly on stage at the Théâtre du Châtelet in Paris during a rehearsal of *Le Bourgeois gentilhomme*, exactly as Molière had died.

Next to my desk I have a rare drawing by Roger Planchon himself. It is a sketch for a play by Arthur Adamov (1908–70). The drawing is an early idea for the staging, showing a railway station and a mound-like rock made out of chopped-up piece of bright blue electric wire, and in its middle is an artificial bed as the centrepiece of the story and to the side a real bed, its actual counterpart. The sketch is simple – Roger never had a lesson of drawing in his life – but it clearly shows the basic elements of the performance space.

When I was at the Théâtre National Populaire (TNP), the company had a discussion with Roger Planchon and someone asked: *Is an idea at all interesting?* To which Roger replied: *There are really only four ideas in the world: Where do people come from? What do they do in the space? Where do they go? And what do we think about it?* And I was baffled: *Really?* I thought – and those questions reminded me of my own childhood as the holder of the T-square questioning Uncle Henry. When someone came with an idea that didn't entirely work, Planchon would say: *C'est intérressant, mais c'est pas beau* (That's interesting but it's not beautiful). There is something more important than ideas, for ideas fade. Something else needs to carry them and give them life. When one makes a piece of work or when one makes music, the desire is to engender what I call a critical debate: What would you want to say *about* this? If there's nothing to say and all one can say is *Oh*, then it's probably not worth the paper it's written on. Sometimes when I worked with directors, I used to think that the programme notes were more interesting than what was on stage. I remember directors talking for hours and hours about concepts and ideas – some of which made it to the programmes but little of it to the stage. Planchon was brilliant in what he called painting pictures with people and in his work everything turned around the person, the human in the middle, rather than the idea. Sometimes having a brilliant idea is not a sufficient justification for art. *Show me something that's beautiful* – no matter if it's an idea or not.

In the 1970s, when Planchon was writing his original plays, I learned all the fundamentals of theatre-making. In one of the scenes of a play, there was an old lady lying in a little wooden bed, dying. Just before she died, the old lady, who was hardly able to move from her bed – wonderfully played by the actress – reached under the bed and found her wooden clogs, her *sabots*. She carefully wrapped a piece of paper underneath so that the *sabots* made no dirt and put them up on a shelf above her head. Then she laid down and said: *C'est bien. C'est tout.* (That's good. That's all.) The clogs are left for the next generation – and it was the most beautiful moment. That wasn't an 'idea' about death, just showing what people did in the Ardèche region in their traditions. Making it clear and plain to an audience – that's beautiful. Such moments stay in one's memory forever.

This is not to say that there is one taste or that people should try to imitate others or be like me – not at all. But beauty is important – even in the smallest, everyday details. I may see two small purple flowers and see that if I placed them on either side of my window, they will give me pleasure. They will die, but they will give me pleasure. Or making a card of condolences: How can I say I am sorry and at the same time give a bit of pleasure? Once a card that I drew simply says, *A message for you*, to which I can write something personal. It is about death, and it shows the earth and air. The people who will receive it might be in distress or need help – and they read the message and understand it without explaining. This is not an idea, but it is beautiful. That's how I try to think in all my compositions.

In 1980, now a single mother of two girls, working at home in a makeshift 'studio' converted from a bedroom, I heard about an extraordinary event at the Nederlands Dans Theater in Amsterdam. The choreographer from Czechoslovakia, Jiří Kylián, had created a new dance piece in homage to his compatriot, composer Leoš Janáček (1854–1928). This new work entitled *Sinfonietta* was said by music and dance critics to be *a milestone in contemporary choreography*, and I determined to go and see it. Through the kindness of a Dutch friend, I obtained a ticket for the final dress rehearsal and somewhere to stay. I sat in a near-empty auditorium in the late afternoon. Suddenly the lights came up, and six trumpeters from the orchestra arrived on stage right – and those trumpets sounded the first thrilling notes of *Sinfonietta*. The dancers came on, and I saw the perfect synthesis of sound, colour and movement. I dreamt of one day making a work like this, little knowing at that time the importance of dreams and that they can come true – albeit unexpectedly.

In 2009, I received an invitation to come back to the National Theatre, Brno, in the Czech Republic to direct and design the world premiere of the first version of Leoš Janáček's opera *The Excursion of Mr Brouček to the Moon* as part of the 2010 *Janáček versus Expressionism* Festival. This was the first production to include the hitherto unperformed Epilogue and of course took me into the cosmic world of the Moon. By sheer coincidence, in February 2010, the Tate Modern Gallery in London opened an exhibition called *Van Doesburg and the International Avant-Garde*. The Dutch multidisciplinary visual artist Theo van Doesburg (1883–1931) was known as 'The Cosmic Occultist', and his work contained overtones of Free Masonic mystery. When I saw the exhibition, I realised what a gift to me it was. The cosmic world of van Doesburg's paintings was exactly how I wished to visualize the lunar world of *Brouček*.

My early training in music when I dreamt of being a classical pianist and my subsequent music exams have in fact stood me in good stead. Thanks to it I know how to read a score, work with an orchestra, talk to conductors and musicians – and I love working with singers. When I received the piano version of the opera, I began to learn it on the keyboard and heard again the voice of my piano teacher – *more staccato! now legato please*. I realised that Janáček had written this like a Viennese waltz, which is in essence a circular dance, and the final part of the score actually is a waltz. Then I remembered a dreamlike situation that I saw several years previously in front of the open-air café at the Výstaviště Exhibition Grounds in Prague – at that time the home of the Prague Quadrennial, the world festival of scenography and performance design. The drawing in my arsenal – my sketchbook – showed this scene: In the deep winter, couples in snow boots and overcoats looking dreamily into each other's eyes, remembering times past and waltzing to a small band with accordions and trumpets.

Then I had a *huge* surprise – the incidence of coincidences: When we started rehearsals for *Brouček*, I saw many new people in the auditorium speaking in, as it sounded, Dutch. It was the Nederlands Dans Theater, and they were going to perform *Sinfonietta* with Jiří

Kylián's choreography and some new video sequences before my production of Janáček's opera. I could hardly believe it! But sure enough, at the first rehearsal six members of the orchestra appeared on stage right, and their trumpets did sound. It was thrilling. I looked to see if Jiří Kylián was with the group. A stage manager directed me to the assistant choreographer, who was charming and told me that Jiří Kylián was not well enough to come, but if I wrote a message, she would give it to him. When she saw the dress rehearsal of *The Excursions of Mr Brouček to the Moon*, she came to me and said: *I felt I was in Brouček's dream myself!* – which was exactly my aim. Moreover, I heard the wonderful sounds of *Sinfonietta* every day of the festival. When it was all over, I donated my maquette of *Brouček* to the Janáček Museum situated in his house in Smetanova Street, which was built in the garden of Janáček's organ school. It was just as though Leoš and Zdenka had gone out for a walk as everything was in its place – the music placed on the piano: a home and not a museum.

The two-part evening that presented Kylián's dance piece to Janáček's *Sinfonietta* and my own production of *Brouček* worked wonderfully together. One critic wrote appreciatively:

Jaroslav Březina sings and plays Brouček with his dark-coloured tenor voice, with shrewd undertones, and also with composure in all the dream and life situations. [. . .] The scene and the sound always come together as allies in this human comedy that makes us laugh but during which no one gets laughed at. That is a dream.

(Gruhl 2010; translation PD)

The experience of making this production was a huge challenge but became a true milestone in my artistic life. Theo van Doesburg's cosmic art served as the perfect visual metaphor that brought together music, poetry and the visual arts in the interplay of opposites that build the world of Janáček's opera about Brouček's brief excursion to the Moon from the realistic, bourgeois life in Prague. Everything in the opera has its counterpart: it is winter on Earth but summer on the Moon; Prague is black and white, but the lunar Temple of Art is full of colours; the students and regulars of the Vikárka pub in Prague are meat-eaters, but Brouček discovers to his astonishment that the people on the Moon are vegetarians. In order to achieve these opposites, I needed to draw every detail very accurately so that the makers in the workshops who were realizing my sketches knew for certain what they had to build.

This production taught me a great deal. I was fortunate to be the first person to stage the Epilogue of Janáček's *Brouček*, bringing together a world of opposites in a cosmic circular dance – a waltz of Janáček's music, the visual poetry of van Doesburg and the world of the drunk meat-eater Matěj Brouček. The work on this opera moved my art of making theatre to another level. (Full details of this production can be found in Howard 2011.)

When I walk through Prague or Brno and see those metal signs of anthropomorphic pigs hanging outside restaurants, dressed up as farmers, cooks or even, once I saw, a ballet dancer, it reminds me of the production. I remember walking through the city with a vegetarian friend one day, looking and asking a waiter standing at a door if he knew anywhere for a vegetarian to eat: *Ah, madame,* he said sadly. *You must know you are in the Land of the Dead Pig.*

In 2014, I was faced with a dilemma that ended up as another milestone of my artistic life. I was asked to create a new production of Bizet's opera *Carmen* – and my initial reply was: *Why would anyone want to do another production of* Carmen? *Haven't we all seen enough?* I always imagined that 'success' was realizing something you had dreamt all your life of doing and even planned, and this was quite the contrary. Rocc, the artistic director of the National Opera in Ljubljana, Slovenia, was extremely patient with me, and simply asked me to listen to Bizet's music and to call him back. I started to listen and watch videos of other productions including Peter Brook's sparse version at Les Bouffes du Nord in Paris, and the ballet *Car-Men* – and I began to feel I possibly had something to offer. I read the book by the anthropologist Prosper Merimée, who had been searching for Greek ruins in the mountains of Andalucia and had come across the story of La Carmencita, who had come from 'outside' (Navarre) and was working in the tobacco factory. Most importantly, I knew and loved the new book by Yaron Matras, *I Met Lucky People: The Story of the Romani Gypsies* (2014). Matras notes that at least 100,000 Roma were killed by the Nazis in a period called 'The Great Devouring' – and yet their culture survives. Then a review in the *Financial Times* weekend Arts page (6 March 2015) of *The Gypsies' Tale* by Garth Cartwright, reported on a Romani brass band called Fanfare Ciocarlia that had been launched into the worldwide spotlight from a Moldavian village. And so the arsenal of the dream of *Carmen* started to fill up. Finally, I remembered how many years ago while travelling by car with a friend outside Seville I had seen a Blue Madonna on a farm cart, piled high with oranges, and with devotional candles round her feet – and I had stopped to draw her. I found the drawing in my memory box and looked again at it, and my decision was made. I rang Rocc, accepted the invitation and asked at the same time if they could invite the wonderful choreographer and dancer from Barcelona Berta Vallribera, who I had always wanted to work with – and the deal was done.

At the time of its opening in 1875, *Carmen* was shocking for French audiences at the Opéra-Comique in Paris, for its 'realistic' approach, considered avant-garde at that time. Bizet asked for the chorus to act convincingly as individuals, rather than respond in unison as a group, and I resolved to find a way to do this. To give each chorus member individuality, I started to create what I call *thinking drawings*. Each evening after rehearsals, I made a pencil drawing of what choreographer Berta and I planned for the next day. I went in early to the opera house to the copy machine and printed enough copies for every member of the chorus to have their own drawing, identify themselves as one of the individuals and maintain that personage. I was amazed how effective that was. Berta's guideline to the whole *Carmen* company was to capture *la duende*, the very heart or spirit that moves a person to sing or dance as an expression of that spirit – whether in joy or in pain. She would say: *We must all try to find the way a person stands, moves and walks – their history. All this is very important for everyone on the stage. There is not one second that anyone can suddenly go into 2015!* The combination of Berta's search for *la duende* and my thinking drawings succeeded in giving each chorus singer individuality – a unique sense of purpose within the grand scheme of Bizet's opera *Carmen*.

Everybody has a different method but the way I start each project is by making a character chart. The left-hand column shows the characters who are in it, one character per line, and each following column is one scene. I make copies for all the cast so that in this chart every actor can usefully see which scenes they are in and what

CARMEN 2015
ENTRACTE
PROPOSAL...

FROM THE MOUNTAIN HIDEOUT A GRAND-
MOTHER TRIES TO TAKE HER GRAND-
CHILDREN TO SAFETY......

they are doing there. This is also a chart that the entire creative team needs – the costume supervisor or the props stage manager – so that we all sing from the same hymn sheet. The chart gives the rhythm and is immensely useful in planning, organization and preparation. Most important, the chart saves time for everyone.

The brilliance of Bizet's work is that all of this also resides in the music. For that reason above all, *Carmen* has been and will continue to be one of the post popular operas ever – despite the fact that it is like a Greek tragedy of destiny and fate. This was the milestone piece of work I least wanted to do, and the one I learned most from, and it is as alive now in my memory as it was when we created it. I am ever grateful.

"ONLY TWO SMALL CHAIRS.."

During the Second World War, in the North of England, I lived with my mother and my maternal grandparents. I was a lonely only child, spending much of the days with my grandparents, while my mother was at work in her uncle's dress-making business, Floral Gowns. My father was conscripted to the army and sent to Egypt before I was born – and I had no concept what a father was. I looked forward each day to the sirens going at night, when we all had to rush to the underground Anderson Shelter. There at least it was fun, with singing and stories, until the 'All Clear' sounded, and I reluctantly went back to my bed in the house. My grandfather had been a cabinetmaker, and he was adept at making things out of old bits of wood – even chairs and eventually bedroom furniture and tables. I did not have conventional toys, apart from a white cuddly dog and an old teddy bear. There were two chairs in the house, painted in different colours, and I used to make up stories that they were doors or castles or gates, and hide behind them and jump out to give everyone a shock.

I have always been in love with chairs – small or large; from Brazil, where they are carved from palm trees; from Beijing, where they are an art form. I have the two small chairs that Rajesh Westerberg made for Chekhov's *The Cherry Orchard* on either side of my fireplace. I created performances in Sao Paulo just with chairs. (See also *What is Scenography?*, pp. 165–7.) And when my grandchildren were small, chairs also became stages to stand on and perform. I became an avid reader of theatre history and poetry. I was given a book of poetry by the then unknown to me Bertolt Brecht, and I read his poem 'About a Painter'. Brecht dedicated this poem to his old school friend Caspar Neher (1897–1962), who was in the German army and deep in the trenches during the First World War. From there, he painted beauty from a small box of watercolours, on paper that his friend Bertolt had sent him. The poem has stayed with me as an artistic landmark ever since. Then I found two more volumes and kept thinking and dreaming that one day I would find and meet these people, not having the faintest idea how. In 1965, I had the good fortune to meet Brecht's translator John Willett, who had just published Brecht's book *The Messingkauf Dialogues*. He gave me a copy and asked if I knew of the painter Caspar Neher, instructing me to read above all this passage:

With what care he selects a chair, and with what thought he places it! And it all helps the playing. One chair will have short legs, and the height of the accompanying table will also be calculated, so that whoever eats at it has to take up a quite specific attitude. (Brecht 1965: 85)

I read the passage, and I knew I had to know more about it – and I had to go and see this theatre! But how?

At this time, John Bury (1925–2000), known as the 'brutalist designer' for his work with Joan Littlewood at the Theatre Royal Stratford East, was appointed head of Design at the nascent National Theatre sited at the Old Vic Theatre in Waterloo. The offices of the National were on the other side of Waterloo Bridge, housed in sheds in Aquinas Street. The secretary to the board was a forceful ex-Girton College woman called Yolande Bird (1922–2016), who described herself as 'an internationalist'. Not coincidentally, the British centre for the International Organisation of Scenographers, Theatre Architects and Technicians (OISTAT) was also running from this office; reciprocal international meetings were organized, and John Bury became its president. An international meeting of theatre technicians from both sides of the Iron Curtain took place in the German Democratic Republic in Berlin, and I was invited to come along as a 'helper'. We drove in a hired bus and eventually found our hotel – the Lokomotiv – and got accommodated after much waiting while the tour organizer searched vainly through unmarked files to find our bookings. I thought it was rather optimistic for world peace that they were so disorganized. The next day, I sat through endless lectures by old German men describing how many screws were in the wooden floor of the new opera house and other such essential bits of knowledge. In the meantime, I read guide books to Berlin hidden on my knees. In the evening, we had a visit to Brecht's theatre – to see the famous Berliner Ensemble. It was thrilling to enter and see the front curtain with Picasso's emblem of the Dove of Peace. Brecht's dictum to his company was, *What has to be done is to develop two arts: an art of acting, and an art of watching.* The next day, instead of going to more lectures about screws and floorboards, I took myself off to the Brecht Archive near the theatre, part of the Academy of the Arts but formerly the apartment where Bertolt Brecht (1898–1956) and Helene Weigel (1900–71) had lived. Here I was able to access the '*Modell-Bücher*' and study how Caspar Neher, Karl von Appen (1900–81) and later Teo Otto (1904–68) had evolved their work with Brecht and the company by making 'speaking drawings'.

"…. and it all helps the
playing …. "

(adapted from a sketch by Caspar
Neher —
'Der Zerrissone' (Nestroy) Staatsoper
Hamburg 1964)

I was totally entranced and lost all track of time, just getting back to the theatre for that evening's performance of Brecht's play with music by Kurt Weill, *The Threepenny Opera* (*Die Dreigroschenoper*, 1928), adapted from John Gay's eighteenth-century ballad opera *The Beggar's Opera* (1728). The synchronicity of word, music and vision brought together in the simple storytelling of the ballad-singer gave me the direction I would aim for in my future work. After that night's performance, John asked where I had been, and far from him being angry as I expected, he graciously complimented me and said he thought it was a very good use of my time, and I appreciated that.

When I returned home to London, I was most surprised to find that a large packet had been delivered. It contained a beautiful book privately published in Vienna – a signed copy of the three last opera works by Caspar Neher. Inside, in glorious free-flowing pen and ink lines with no frames to the edges of the drawing are his thoughts for each moment and on the pages in different places is just one small boudoir chair, its back like a mirror watching the characters. The final sketchbook, most intense in its simplicity, was for Gottfried von Einem's opera *Der Zerrissene* (1961–4) with Boris Blacher's libretto after a farce by the early nineteenth-century Austrian playwright Johann Nestroy. I made a textile fabric on calico and screen-printed the little chair from Caspar Neher's final sketchbook, in pink and blue, and made curtains for my house. In that way, Caspar Neher and his art of making theatre have become part of my daily life.

In August 1965, the now-established National Theatre of Great Britain housed at the Old Vic invited the Berliner Ensemble to bring four productions to London, among them *The Resistable Rise of Arturo Ui*, *The Threepenny Opera* and *Coriolanus*, in which Brecht's widow Helene Weigel played Volumnia. There was also a special morning performance of *The Little Mahagonny* for theatre professionals and workers, and a public exhibition of the designs and drawings of Karl von Appen. John Bury asked if I would help Weigel and her assistant to hang the exhibition, as rehearsals would have to take priority. Without hesitation I agreed. On the day the Berliner Ensemble arrived, we watched in amazement as three huge transporters rolled up outside the Old Vic stage door (at that time in Waterloo Road). The organization, the unloading and the setting-up was impeccable. But the most impressive was that all the stage crew assigned to stage left wore a green bodyband and the stage right crew wore a red one, and they *never* crossed the centre line. Thus, I met the great Helene Weigel. She was immediately warm and generous to me thanking me before I had done anything. And she began to instruct me in how to hang an exhibition. (See also *What is Scenography?*, pp. 177–8.) To this day I follow her instructions both for my own exhibitions and for those I have also curated for others.

I look very often at those pen and ink drawings of Caspar Neher, and the wonderful flowing lines of the Polish artist Tadeusz Kulisiewicz (1899–1988), who recorded Weigel's performance as *Mother Courage* on their tour of Poland.

In January 1986, I created my first full-performance piece in the empty bar of Riverside Studios – devised, designed and performed by first-year Theatre Design students at the Central School of Art and Design, where I was head of Theatre. It was part of the Arts Council Exhibition *Caspar Neher – Brecht's Designer.* I called the production *About a Painter – a non-sequential view of the life and work of Theatre Designer Caspar Neher.* It caught the imagination of many of my contemporaries: choreographer Stuart Hopps, composer Carl Davis, the costume specialist Ann Curtis, and the actor Alec McCowen (1925–2017), and we still talk about it when we meet.

I never discovered who had sent the book to me, but it lives in the precious corner of my library. It came at the right moment – as a mysterious serendipity – when I returned from my first trip to East Berlin. Who sent the book will probably always remain a mystery but I have my suspicions and gratitude – to John Bury, Helene Weigel and many others. Not least: Thank you John Willett (1917–2002) for seeing a direction in which to push me – for I think you sent me that book, with Caspar Neher's sketches for little chairs on the stage.

Chairs have always been an indelible part of who I am as a theatre-maker. From a childhood memory, so many years ago in that small council house in Newcastle upon Tyne, I remember a rhyme taught to me by my aunt, who was a teacher. The children I knew in our community did not get 'presents' but got a certificate to say they had been given a tree in the Promised Land:

Two little chairs are looking at you . . .
One is pink and one is blue!
Stand on the blue and you will see

A land far away where you have a tree!
Stand on the pink one and you will know
What goes on in the earth below . . .

One day, as I was talking to a friend about the synchronicity of
life, serendipity and the art of making theatre, someone threw an
unsigned card through my letterbox. It only had the following
poem on it:

The more one *looks*,
The more one *sees*.
The more one *sees*,
The more one *imagines*.
The more one *imagines*,
The more one *invents*.
The more one *invents*,
The more one *creates*.

It must be by someone who knows me very well because this is
my process of work. The importance of looking, seeing, imagining,
inventing and creating, together with the magic of serendipity, is
central to my art of making theatre.

In August 2016, a horrendous fire burnt down the Selsey Academy
with the substantial loss of archives. A local charity, Arts Dream Selsey,
embarked on a community project to retrace some of the memories
of past staff and students who had been part of the academy over the
last fifty years, and to produce an online exhibition of photographs
and stories detailing interesting memories. The second part of the
project was to commission me to use some of the stories and images
as a stimulus for a large-scale artwork to be displayed in a variety of
venues around the Manhood Peninsula in West Sussex. The project
received support from the National Lottery Heritage Fund. As for the
artwork I created, it started off as a coincidence – like so many others.
I was walking down the High Street in Selsey past a local shop selling
fridges that had recently been delivered. There were big cardboard
boards from the packing outside the shop. One side of the board
came away, and I noticed that inside the board was paper folded
in a honeycomb pattern, which sparked my interest. I didn't know
exactly why, but it was somehow appealing: on the outside it looked
like one thing but on the inside it was completely another – with a

hidden world in it. I went into the shop and asked if they wanted the board. They not only didn't but they also gave me another four. That's how the project started.

I began to cut into the board and started making the visual composition from the texture, telling the story of Selsey Academy from the 1960s up to the fire in 2016. The serendipity of the creative process continued. In one corner I wanted to create trees, as they were on the grounds of the school, but I didn't want to simply draw them. And then I was cleaning one of my plastic palettes after using green acrylic paint, and the dried paint peeled off. I would have normally thrown it away, but it attracted my attention with its texture and suggested itself as the material for the trees. The result was very satisfactory – and it came from looking at it and seeing how I could use it. Another method I used in the mural was a technique we were taught when I was an art student in 1954: how to stretch paper by soaking and fixing it with butterfly tape (brown sticky paper) on a drawing board. To picture the part of Selsey Academy that didn't burn down – the art room – I used the gum paper from the side of my drawing board which I have had since my student days. This was to convey the idea of the art room without saying it in words. The material itself has the power of telling the story.

The resulting mural is tactile – like much of my work – because I want people to touch it and feel the textures as they are all part of the story. Making tactile artwork has become increasingly important as the population gets older and sight gets weaker. So, when people come to my exhibitions, they can experience the work in many ways – seeing it, listening to it and touching it. It gives them a full and multisensory enjoyment of the art.

What I do in my studio I don't think of as *work* at all. I call it *life*. I have one life in my house and one life in my studio. My friend in France would call it *la création*, which suits it better than *work*. I am very fortunate to have my home separate from my studio. It keeps the two lives distinct and allows me to enjoy both to the full. Keeping a system and an order to things makes *la création* not only possible but also gives it a greater focus. I also force myself to file everything to maintain the system, although I hate filing – because unless I do, I won't be able to find it. Now, all my *work* things are in the studio and all my *home* things are in the house – never the twain shall meet. I find the separation of the two activities – my home and my professional, artistic practice – important for my progression. Of course, until I had a house with a studio, I worked in converted bedrooms – all the work I did at the National Theatre, at the Birmingham Rep or at the Royal Shakespeare Company was done in tiny confined spaces. Still, no matter where one works, separating home life from professional work is crucial and productive.

One of the things I've learned since I was a child is that no matter what one is doing, it is important to find the right height in the right space and in the right spatial arrangement. There is a different height necessary to cut things so that one uses the full power of their arm, and there is a different height to make drawings. Because I am right handed, I need to have all my colour pencils and paints by my right hand. Also, different projects are dedicated different spaces, and if I am working on one project, I can also see the other. How we organize our space is very important as it helps the resulting work.

When I moved to my own house in Selsey, I realised how much having a dedicated studio means. The single thing that made an absolute difference in my life is creating my own space. When I was an art student in Birmingham and at the Slade in London, each of us had their own workstation – a space like a box where one could pin up pictures and concentrate the creative work. It had a light, and there was a locker underneath. That's where one could make a model of their design. The teacher would come and talk with the student about it. As far as I know, things are very different now, and only few art schools still have individual stations. But having a dedicated workspace of one's own is very important, especially for artists.

When I mention to others that I work in my studio every day or that I don't have time on a certain day, they are surprised. They assume that I have retired – and the concept that I should have retired is truly prevalent. People expect that others should have hobbies, but I don't think I've had a hobby in my life or time for one. They are often surprised that the professional work you do can be so fulfilling.

If I have a pastime, I write poems – sometimes for friends, like this one for Michael Kustow when he was dying:

TO THOSE WHO DIE ALONE
For Michael Kustow

She held his hand, he held her hand
Over the thin white sheet
That was too hot for him to bear,
Over the motorway of tubes and wires
Criss-crossing the tormented vibrating bed.

She would not let him go
Spiralling down the vortex
Towards the plug hole.
And he could not go
Because although his huge body
Was skeletal and wasted,
His shoulders were too broad
To slip easily down
And he would not leave her.

They shared the battle.
But what happens to those that die alone
And have no reason to fight
In the darkness of the night
When all sense of time and space is lost?

LOCKED DOORS & HIDDEN SECRETS

The great fortune in my artistic life has been the privilege of the mentorship of the great designer Jocelyn Herbert, whom I had met when I was an art student in Birmingham and went to see the Arnold Wesker trilogy at the Belgrade Theatre in Coventry. Jocelyn took an interest in my work and frequently invited me to come to her home in North West London with my portfolio. She would look carefully and make acute suggestions, often as to what I could leave out. Jocelyn was a friend of the great theatre designer Tatiana (Tanya) Benita Moiseiwitsch (1914–2003), daughter of the famous pianist Benno Moiseiwitsch. Tanya worked very closely with the Irish director Tyrone Guthrie (1900–71), who conceived the architecture of the so-called Guthrie theatres that reintroduced the thrust stage – at Stratford, Ontario and the Guthrie Theatre, Minneapolis. In 1962, Guthrie came to Chichester to speak publicly to the people of Chichester in the council's Assembly Rooms and convince them that the 'thrust stage' was the only way forward for the dawning of the New Age of making theatre. On that impulse, the Chichester Festival Theatre was built, modelled on the other 'Guthrie' theatres. In 1984, Jocelyn was invited to this theatre to design a new production of Shakespeare's *The Merchant of Venice*, directed by Patrick Garland (1935–2013), with Alec Guinness (1914–2000) playing Shylock and Joanna MacCallum as Portia. Jocelyn called me, saying she did not think she would be free to do this and asked if she could propose me in her place? I was astonished, fearful and thankful, and as soon as the theatre agreed, I began the research – to create the story I had read and even memorized – the play I had dreamt that one day I would put my own imprint upon. I knew only too well what it was like to be forced to wear a yellow circle or star to be easily identified and had heard many stories as a child from those who had escaped from a ghetto in Europe. I went to meet the great actor Alec Guinness and told him I planned to go to Venice to the ghetto. He took me to his study and showed me his collection of paintings by the still-life painter Giorgio Morandi (1890–1964), and pointed out one of them: a shelf with jugs – but there was one jug facing in the opposite direction: black, while the others were white and cream. *That's what this play is about*, he said – and I remembered.

I went to Venice with my daughter and a sketchbook, and found my way to the old Ghetto and saw a small brass plaque in Latin stating the Rules of the Ghetto when it was set up in 1516.

RULES OF THE VENICE GHETTO
1516
ALL JEWS MUST LIVE INSIDE
THIS GHETTO ~ NO EXCEPTIONS

THESE WALLS WILL BE
GATED AND LOCKED AT DUSK
EACH NIGHT

ANY JEWS FOU TSID WILL BE
ARRE ED
ALL JEWS ER THE
YELLOW IRCLE

ALL RULES COMPULSORY

OFFENCES PUNISHABLE
BY ORER

The Ghetto had its three crucial characteristics. Firstly, it was compulsory that every Jew without exception had to live inside the Ghetto. Secondly, the Ghetto was enclosed in walls and gates and was to be locked at night, allegedly as a safety measure. And thirdly, the Ghetto was to be segregated from other religious communities – no Christians were allowed to live inside. Strict financial regulations and fines were in place to force the inhabitants of Venice to comply. The word *ghetto* literally means *foundry* – a place for smelting copper, an ironic metaphor for the gas ovens yet to come. The Jews of Venice were forced to be contained within the walls 'for their own safety', and today we know that containment is a euphemism for imprisonment.

I passed through the iron gates and looked at the tall thin buildings, and I knew just what I was going to do. I would find an English translation of the Latin, and for my design of *The Merchant of Venice* make a large wall with the writing cut into the wall – as is done in tombstones. I thought the wall could swing open for the court-room scene and the scenes that take place in Belmont. Alec asked for a small side door that he could enter through, trailing his gabardine, before starting the scene. The play resonated with many events across the world. The 1980s, when we were working on the production, was the time of the Apartheid in South Africa, of walls being built in California to keep Mexicans out or the wall in Gaza between Israel and Jordan – and the wall in our production became the visual metaphor for the play and the state of the world. The drawing included here is the first sketch I made for Alec on my return from Venice. Shylock wears his compulsory gabardine of plain black with the obligatory yellow circle, but the lining of this garment is a beautiful hand-embroidered cloth from Japan I found in a London street market. Alec (as Shylock) said this made him feel as though he kept his wealth close to his body, and this is a good example how clothes can tell a story and help an actor. (The model, Guinness's costume for Shylock and all my drawings are in the Theatre Collection of the Victoria and Albert Museum in London.)

The Venice Ghetto today is well described by the master potter, artist and author Edmund de Waal in an article in *The Guardian* (24 April 2019). Giving an account of his experience making an artwork called *The Library of Exile and Loss*, he describes the Venetian square in the Campo di Ghetto Nuovo still redolent of memories as a very special place despite its seeming normality. There is no church, there are no public buildings and there are no grand thresholds with runs of stairs. And as I saw myself, there is a sense of enclosure even though the gates now stand open. There are five taller arched windows in one wall and a domed skylight you can see through one of the windows – an indication that this was the site of a former synagogue. A stone embedded into a wall, engraved in Hebrew, bears an inscription from Psalm 32:

> Many sorrows shall be to the wicked: but he that trusts in the LORD, mercy shall surround him. (NKJV, Psalm 32.10)

And above the stone, a tablet higher up on the wall commemorates the deportations of Jews in 1943.

Since my childhood in Newcastle upon Tyne, I have always hated walls. At the bottom of our street was the Roman Hadrian's Wall, which separated Scotland from England. Perhaps because I am a typical Capricorn, when I see or feel a wall I immediately think I have to force my way through it, often with harmful consequences. I rarely notice that there is a nearby door that could be opened. In my small bedroom, I didn't have a colourful picture of bunny rabbits; I had a print of people all in black walking by a large wall. I often wondered who they were and where they were going. Many years later, I discovered it was a print by the Lithuanian-American artist Ben Shahn (1898–1969) and depicted immigrants in New York. When I was working on *The Merchant of Venice*, the wall that had accompanied me since my childhood materialized on the stage and with it the tyranny of containment and restrictions to freedom that walls stand for.

I can never thank Jocelyn's generosity enough for giving me that opportunity – especially as I found out later that she was not busy at all.

As a teenager in Birmingham with a small amount of pocket money and living not far from the Stratford Road, I discovered I could get on a Midland Red bus to Stratford upon Avon by way of Henley in Arden, famous for its ice creams. I had just enough money to get off at Henley in Arden and buy an ice cream and then get on the next bus to Stratford. I used to sit on the grass outside the red-brick walls of the theatre and dream that one day I might be able to get in, and possibly even meet the great John Barton (1928–2018), who was creating something called *The Wars of the Roses* – which was not in my Collected Works of William Shakespeare that my elocution teacher had given me. I knew because I had devoured all these amazing plays! One day my teacher heard of my escapades and told me that if I watched when people came out to have a drink on the terrace in the middle of the play – which she said was 'an interval' – I should follow a family, just go in and look for an empty seat. She assured me, *there are always empty seats*. I became an expert at quickly spotting empty seats, and in this way over time I saw many Shakespeare plays – but only the second halves. Still, it was exciting and gave me a determination that one day I would get into those red-brick walls and become part of that world. I had no idea at all how I was going to do that or what I would be able to do when I got there. But I could remember the plays, and that seemed to be a useful start.

Walls are not only visible. The most difficult walls to break through are those we can't see. In 2002, I received an invitation from Georgi Aleksi-Meskhishvili to a residency at Dartmouth College, Hanover, United States. The residency gave me the opportunity to create a new production at the Hopkins Centre for the Arts – a public theatre in the town, seating 900 spectators, and with an enormous envelope-like stage. For several years, I had been working with the Hispanist and specialist in medieval drama Robert Potter (1934–2010) from the University of California, Santa Barbara. We had met in 1987 when he was in the UK on a residency at Royal Holloway College in London. I thought at last one of the dreams in my arsenal could be realised. I knew that Dartmouth had a highly regarded Department of Romance Languages and a renowned Music Department, and I hoped they would cooperate on the realization of my dream – a new English version of Fernando de Rojas's Spanish tragicomedy called *La Celestina* (published anonymously in 1499).

A few years earlier, in 1999, we explored *La Celestina* in a week's workshop at the Almeida Theatre in North London. The composer Lucie Skeaping, a specialist in Sephardic music, a group of eminent actors and myself worked on the play and presented our work in one public performance in the theatre. Now the opportunity for a full production – and the realization of a dream – seemed to offer itself.

The world of *La Celestina* is set in the hidden secret world of the *converso* Jews in Spain, living as loyal Catholics, under the tyranny and fundamentalism of King Ferdinand and Queen Isabella. The play was originally written by an anonymous author to be read around a table. It was later revealed that the play was actually written around 1492 by an author who was himself a *converso*: Fernando de Rojas embedded his name in a traditional Jewish acrostic using the letters of his name in a diagonal across the page.

The Prologue describes the play as *A tale of lovers, sweet in the telling, bitter at the core, lascivious and laughable, fit for the hearing of all fellow sufferers – an example to be heeded, a truth to share.* The story of La Celestina – a former actress turned matchmaker – with her mysterious qualities has fascinated translators, authors and especially painters ever since. The French composer Maurice Ohana (1913–92) wrote a lyrical opera *La Célestine* that was only once performed in 1988 at the Palais Garnier in Paris. In 1968, Pablo Picasso (1881–1973) worked on a series of sixty-six copperplate etchings based on the erotic love themes of *La Celestina* – a subject that had interested him throughout his life. On a painting of 1904, made at the end of his 'Blue Period', a once beautiful woman looks out of the canvas – her good eye seeing into the future and the other glass eye looking into the past. Her body is strongly in the present, and she seems to challenge the viewer to speculate about her mystery and her secrets as if to say: *Now I'm worn out and nobody wants me, even though I still have the urge for it. God knows – the only pleasure I've got left is to watch.* This moving portrait of the old one-eyed go-between La Celestina demonstrates Picasso's solidarity with distressed, famished and oppressed humanity, and his great compassion for the poor. The Portuguese artist living in Britain, Paula Rego – promoted by the Tate Gallery as an uncompromising artist of extraordinary imaginative power who revolutionalized the way in which women are represented – created a series of detailed paintings of the world of Celestina's House in 2001, noting that Fernando de Rojas also called it a *Tragicomedia de Calisto y Melibea*. Rego's paintings also reflect the mixed population of Spain at the time.

At Dartmouth, I was dismayed when I saw the auditorium of the Hopkins Centre. It was *huge*. I sat there and thought: *This space is all wrong for this play.* Then the manager of the theatre came to speak to me and asked me if everything was all right. I explained my reservations, and asked if it could be possible to use the auditorium to illuminate Fernando de Rojas' only stage direction which says simply 'A Town by the Sea'. Eventually we reached agreement, and I created a walled garden on the stage space and closed the auditorium, except as a jasmine-scented entrance for the spectators, who entered the closed secret world on the stage through the usually locked proscenium doors.

I wondered how I could create the sea. Looking at the empty rows in the auditorium, which we wouldn't now be using, I thought that maybe I could drape some sheets over them – like dust sheets that are used in the theatre – only blue! My collaborator Joan Morris was a textile specialist and offered to dye the sheets in different shades of blue. But where could we find so many sheets? I wondered if there was a local hospital that had old bed linen to spare. A hospital in Hanover, New Hampshire, had a full store of them, and when I told them why we needed it, they delivered a full van! As the audience entered the auditorium, they saw blue sheets draped all over the regular seating. Little origami white paper boats accented in a rippling light made it clear this was the sea as the spectators were walking through the waves towards the town. To complete the illusion, our Japanese composer Kyoko Kobayashi wrote a wonderful atmospheric electronic score incorporating original music played on the oud from *Ya Ainy* by the Israeli composer and my former student Gaï Gutman. The audience were directed to walk through our sea towards the two proscenium doors and up into another auditorium built on the huge stage.

One day, at Dartmouth College, Georgi took me to the Hood Museum of Art on the university campus, which houses a wonderful collection of paintings by Mark Rothko (1903–70). I learned that this famous American painter was born in Dvinsk, Latvia – where my grandfather was born! Not long after visiting the Rothko exhibition, I was at a theatre conference in Riga, and my host Ilyas Blumberg (1943–2016) took me to Dvinsk. There, in a small local museum, was an archive section, and I found under my father's name, Hoffman, a photograph of a Rothko family wedding – with my paternal grandparents attending as guests of honour!

Rothko's painting *Lilac and Orange* is a prime example of his compositional style – and inspired me to paint the walls of our stage space in bold brushstrokes to represent the town. Characteristically, Rothko's canvases are large in scale and were meant to be seen in relatively close environments so that the viewer was virtually enveloped by the experience when confronted with the work. As the artist wrote, *I paint big to be intimate* – and this was the perfect reference. On three of the walls of the stage space, we put up boards – a terracotta paint smeared with brush strokes painted by the students – and in that way Rothko became an inspiration and a presence in our production of *La Celestina*.

On the huge stage of the Hopkins Centre, the spectators sat on either side of a raised platform with small raked stages at either end representing 'uptown' and 'downtown'. This enabled the production to move swiftly without scene changes from comedy to the final tragedy at the conclusion of the play. The audience were excited and expectant, finding themselves in this new and unusual space so close to the actors. The 'street' that led across the stage between the seated audience had trapdoors – for most of the duration invisible – and actors as they died disappeared through unseen doors behind the audience – as it were to enter the underworld. In the final scene, Melibea's father Pleberio cradles his dead daughter's body in his arms and sadly asks, *For whom did I build towers?* – before revealing his heavy secret that he and his wife Doña Alisa had never told Melibea that she was not a

Spanish Catholic but in fact the daughter of converted Jews. He then embarks on the tragic biblical lament descending into 'This Vale of Tears'. In the final moment of our production, the dead rise from the traps back onto the street and dance a medieval Dance of Death before they disappear again, back to the underworld. A celestial ceiling made of stars – which were in fact old knives and forks that I found in a container of old cutlery in one of Hanover's thrift shops and wired them together to form stars – lit up, and a gentle wind moved them in the sky above the stage space. The audience spontaneously looked up and did not notice the cast reappearing from the underworld to take their final bow.

In the Prologue, Fernando de Rojas speaks directly to the listeners:

> Anyone who seeks true meaning here
> Must look beyond the plot, search for the essence,
> Pondering hints and questions,
> And hidden difficulties –
> For things are never what they seem . . .

Every line and speech contains hidden clues to the true identity of the doomed lovers – like in the secret life of Fernando de Rojas himself. As the listeners uncover the story behind the text, so does the character of the father (who is really de Rojas himself) gradually reveal his true identity as a *converso* Jew. In that way, this play – or novel in dialogue – touches on the great issues of our times. We cannot hide who and what we are, no matter how hard we try. There will always be a moment when our true nationality, religion, gender or sexuality is revealed – and perhaps with some relief. We must face what we are and how we live with ourselves. The intolerance of any society that forces people to deny their origins in order to conform to a totalitarian vision is as abhorrent now as it was in de Rojas's time. And those who tried to be what was required in public while retaining their own identity in secret became pariahs in both camps.

In 2006, I began the realization of a dream when I passed by chance the Royal Academy of Arts in Piccadilly in London and saw a poster. It showed the self-portrait of the young Berlin artist Charlotte Salomon (1917–43) staring out at me. I went into the exhibition, beautifully curated by Monica Bohm-Duchen, and was astounded, for here was a young girl painting for her life. Charlotte Salomon painted 800 gouaches with transparent overlays filled with texts and musical references. She had only three colours – red, yellow and blue – and some watercolour paper and some tracing paper she brought with her to France. Charlotte Salomon invented new names for herself and other people close to her, as if they were the protagonists of a German *singspiel* – self-ironically asking herself as she reviewed her work *Is This Life? or Theatre?* This astounding collection of artworks was made in the last three years of her life when she was sent by her father and her stepmother to her grandparents in Villefranche-sur-Mer in France to escape the Nazi persecution of Jews in Germany. Charlotte's grandparents were already in hiding in a shepherd's hut 'La Bergerie' in the grounds of l'Hermitage owned by the American Ottilie Moore – the saviour of many children during those dark times.

Shortly after I saw the exhibition, the theatre designer Sally Jacobs (1932–2020) gave me the volume of Salomon's paintings published in New York by Viking Press (1981) saying to me: *I know this book should belong to you.* I began serious research into her story, determined to find an alternative to simply projecting her paintings onto a screen as a background to the action. I learned that in 1941 Charlotte's father, Albert Salomon (1883–1976), a former doctor at the Berlin hospital, was released from a concentration camp through the efforts of his wife Paula Lindberg (1897–2000), a famous opera singer at the Berlin Opera House, who was no longer allowed to sing there. The parents managed to survive the war and eventually restored their daughter's artwork. I dreamt of attempting to realise her world in three dimensions: chairs, the recurring theme of the sofa – which was a place of refuge – and her bed covered with a quilt referencing her painting *The Field of Buttercups.*

In 2013, with the librettist and actor Alon Nashman, who had also seen the same exhibition at the Art Gallery of Ontario in Toronto, and the Czech composer Aleš Březina, we began an exploratory workshop on *Charlotte* at Canadian Stage – with stand-in furniture and without any props or costumes. Nashman and I had met in Edinburgh where he was presenting his one-man piece on Kafka, and we decided to be co-creators. Several years before, I had met Aleš Březina, a leading Martinů specialist and the director of the Martinů Institute in Prague, when working on Martinů's opera *The*

Greek Passion in Thessaloniki. As I was walking through Toronto, I noticed across the street a large building site, and I saw a building truck delivering planks of wood, all wrapped in plastic sheets. We, one of the theatre technicians and I, asked them if we could have the sheets, which they happily gave us. I saw that the plastic sheets could represent the sheets of tracing paper that Charlotte put over her gouaches. In the Canadian Stage workshop, we laid them flat on the ground, mixed up some latex paints in red, yellow and blue, and with large dry brushes spattered the paint onto the sheets as if it was no more than the marks of where a painting had been. The stage we were working on had a three-sided balcony, and we hung the sheets from them – and immediately could see we had created two worlds: a reality and a memory.

Our 'Tri-Coloured Play with Music' developed over many years, but I wanted to recreate a few simple pieces of real furniture like Charlotte drew them – and thought perhaps out of cardboard – but could not find anyone to do this. I was talking to a neighbour about my problem, and she reminded me that she worked in interior design and has made furniture for hotels. She said: *Draw what you think you want and come with me to Vilnius in Lithuania next week where I am going to see how my new consignment is coming along* and then added those magic words: *I will arrange everything.* And so in a few days after this, I was on a flight to Kaunas, the nearest airport to Vilnius. The furniture manufacturer Karolis came to meet us in his van and had booked us accommodation at a beautiful small hotel adjacent to the Old Town.

On our first morning in Vilnius, I was free, as they had business to do, so I thought I would walk through the Old Town. It was a sunny spring day, and under the baroque archway two heavy iron gates were open. I wondered why the Old Town had such gates, and then I saw people prostrating themselves on the ground and looking up at a Madonna in a high window in the centre of the arch. She was surrounded by lit candles and tears of pearls were streaming from her eyes. I began to walk through a small winding street wondering where I really was. Then I remembered that Vilnius had belonged to Poland and was called Vilna, the notorious walled ghetto. In the Vilna ghetto, during the Second World War, all the Jews were exterminated except for a few that had dug a secret tunnel under the walls and hid in the forest of Baltic pine trees between Vilna and Kaunas. Then I saw on an old brick wall in the street with a gold brick in Lithuanian and English, confirming that I was indeed walking in the main street of that infamous place.

At midday, Karolis and my neighbour Beverley came to fetch me and took me to his workshop. We had a light lunch in the lovely modern restaurant in the hotel, but I kept quiet about my morning. They were both cheerful and excited to know what my reaction to the prototype of Charlotte's chair would be. We began the drive, and after we left the town, in the direction of Kaunas, I saw we were going along the side of a forest where several trees had been felled. It flashed through my head that this could have been the forest where the twenty people hid. I suppressed the idea as a fantasy. We arrived at the workshop – and there was a full-size version of Charlotte's chair, of course unpainted. I was speechless as I began to realise this must have been made from the trees in the very forest where the escapees from the Vilna ghetto had hidden. I asked Karolis if he knew anything about this and was astonished as he had never heard of the Vilna ghetto and this story. But there was an old man working there who overheard my question and spoke good English. He came over to me and said: *You are quite right – and indeed your furniture is made from these trees. Karolis is young, and we keep silent – for this history is a hidden secret now.*

Some events are so incredible that I doubt whether they are true or a dream.

Several years later, during the Covid-19 pandemic lockdown, I gave a talk about this story for Head Held High, a charity that organizes cultural events mainly for elderly people in care homes. As part of the talk, I was showing the pictures of my chairs and from our production. After the talk on Zoom, one woman came forward and said she knew the story and everything about the forest. Her family came from Vilna, and her father was one of the two men who managed to escape when the twenty men were captured in the forest. I cannot express my astonishment at the coincidence. It was all true. Ultimately, our production of *Charlotte* has been lauded as a success, but the backstory that gained validity so serendipitously, thanks to this woman, remains an incredible mystery.

When I was working at the Central Academy in Beijing on the project *The Metaphysical World of the Tyrant King Macbeth* (2017), the organizers concluded the event by hosting a 'forum'.

INSIDE THE LOCKED GATES OF thE VILNA GHETTo

I had no idea what that could be, but when the day came, they said that there would be about 400 people in the theatre who had come for the 'forum' from all around China to ask me questions about *What is Scenography?* I had had no idea that this was coming but I did my best to respond. At the end of the event, one of the persons came to me and asked if he could talk to me. He introduced himself in very good English as the head of the Theatre Academy in Shanghai and invited me to come. I had always dreamed of going to Shanghai and knew something of its history. He then offered to show me remarkable moments of Shanghai's history – such as the story of 30,000 émigrés from Nazi Europe who were welcomed to his city during the Second World War. Shanghai has always been international and retained its unique cultural identity, separate from mainland China – ever since old silk merchants from hundreds of years ago came from the Caucasus Mountains and all along the Silk Road. Some of them married Chinese women and became Chinese. In the Old Town, behind the old synagogue, which is now a museum, there is a huge bronze metal wall with the names of every family that had ever come to Shanghai engraved on it. The visit to Shanghai was one of the most memorable trips of my entire life and showed me unknown stories of locked doors and hidden secrets.

The Prague Quadrennial (PQ) – the festival of Scenography and Performance Design that has been held in Prague every four years since 1967 – has always been a unique opportunity for meeting people, at the time of the Iron Curtain that separated the East from the West, as well as nowadays when new invisible walls appear. The festival brings together artists and cultures from all around the world, opening doors between them. That's where we can not only meet but also get inspiration. It has been a great privilege for me to be involved in it. There I met the German scenographer and stage director Achim Freyer, who had just done Wagner's *The Ring Cycle* and the Mozart trilogy acting jointly on the productions as a director and visual creator. That meeting opened a door that had been locked to me: it inspired me to follow his path and combine scenography and directing.

Another wonderful person I met at PQ was Bentzie Munitz, a phenomenal lighting designer from Tel Aviv. When he retired in 2013, I went to the celebration of his life, wrote an anonymous acrostic poem in his honour – not unlike the acrostic that opens Fernando de Rojas's *La Celestina*. During the event, I had a hundred copies handed out to the guests:

BRIGHT LIGHT SHINING . . .

Bright light shining
Ever kind & generous
Never showing off
Teaching people skills
Zooming over continents
International symbol
Entertaining friends
Mildly amused by others
Unimpressed by officials
Novel ideas
Introduced with tact
To open people's minds
Zoned into creativity

This is our friend we celebrate today

As part of the Prague Quadrennial 2007, we organized a critical series entitled Top Ten Talks, financed by Stanford University. Ten world-leading theatre makers – among them the German composer and theatre director Heiner Goebbels, the Polish theatre-maker Krystyna Meissner, the multidisciplinary theatre artist Mariaelena Roqué, and the Canadian scenographer Michael Levine – were invited to Prague to give their talks. Another programme that had started at PQ 2003 was the Student Exhibition. In 2007, we invited the participating design schools to do something different. We asked them to work on a common project called *A Lear for Our Times* and bring scale models and drawings how to stage Shakespeare's *King Lear* innovatively. The idea behind this was to use *King Lear* as a shared artistic language to build relationships between students from different cultures. In 2007, we also decided to make connections between the Student Exhibition and the Top Ten Talks – and we gave the invited renowned speakers a special task. Every morning at nine, I went to fetch each of them from their hotel and took them to the Student Exhibition. There we involved them in the discussions of the student maquettes for *King Lear* – and that turned into a fantastic experience for everyone. After the discussion, we all went to a café to have a cup of coffee with the students – a part of the schedule that was absolutely mandatory. The guest speakers then had a car ready to take them to the airport to catch their planes back home. This initiative had a very important function: the theatre-makers had to be there as an authority in their field and also as a social person. That experience had immense value and significance for the participating students – having people like Heiner Goebbels talking to them at close quarters, having coffee together and discussing their work opened doors for many aspiring artists and allowed us all to participate in the hidden secrets of the art of making theatre.

A NEW USE FOR OLD TABLE-CLOTHS

During the Second World War – a time of crisis when food was rationed – slow cooking became the norm. Soup was advocated as an energy-saving method of survival, along with 'Digging for Victory' – families growing vegetables, especially carrots, which allegedly allowed people to see in the dark when the blackouts were enforced. As a small child, I used to walk with my grandfather to his allotment. I carried a torch with a black hood over it so that we could just see our feet. We fell over quite a lot. In our tiny kitchen, there were two wooden barrels – one with cucumbers being pickled and one for pickling herrings. The smell was overpowering. From the ceiling hung pots and pans, spoons and ladles that made music clashing together when the windows were open. The coal fire in the sitting room was also an oven and a stove, and on it a large blue enamel pot of soup bubbled away cooking slowly for hours. Later I came to realise that I had grown up in a theatre of smell, as well as vision and hearing.

My grandmother was a tiny round lady, and my grandfather – a former cabinetmaker – made her a wooden platform out of old bits and pieces of wood he found, so she could stand at the sink and see out of the kitchen window. She knew how to skin a chicken, bone it and stuff the skin, make soup and roast the rest whole – with carrots and onions that made me cry as I watched her dice them. This was wartime, and neighbours exchanged food with each other – a bag of sugar for a slab of butter was commonplace, not to mention dried eggs in tins. A chenille flowered tablecloth covered the dining room table. Later I found that this cloth had carried some of my grandparents' possessions when they had left their small village in Russia to make the journey – as they thought to New York. When my mother married in 1938 just before the war, which took my father away for seven years, the tradition was to give lace or embroidered teatime tablecloths made of linen as wedding presents. Every household had its special drawer of tablecloths that were almost never used. Sometimes I draped tablecloths over our small chairs and made them into houses – and I could sit hidden inside my 'house' and look at my books. Of course, I did not know that all these early impressions are deeply ingrained in our brains for use later on – for in them we all have 'arsenals' where storage and images and events remain until one day the occasion comes to use them.

Many years later, in 1994, when the European Scenography Centres project was launched, Edwin Erminy Bayley (1959–2018),

THE TABLE-CLOTH FRONT
DOORS
RONDO ADAFINA : LONDON 2000

one of the mature students from Caracas, Venezuela, took a year away from his job as director of productions at the Teresa Carreño Opera House. He said he was tired of making other people's work marvellous, and he wanted to make his own work. His scenographic dream was to become both a visual artist and an innovator but primarily a poetic writer – and to adapt Alejo Carpentier's famous magic realist novel *Concierto Barroco* (1974) for the stage. A first version of *Concierto Barroco* was staged as a work in progress in the Lethaby Gallery at the Central School of Art and Design London in 1995 – and a dream began to become a reality. The show was later fully staged in Venezuela and in London.

Sometimes when artists meet, they not only exchange ideas but other, more important things happen, and one wonders what developments can dreams have. Edwin suggested that we form a theatre company and make a piece of work together. A mutual interest from this multicultural group of theatre-makers was to explore cultural identity and the void created by leaving one's country, one's family and one's people for another life. We established our theatre company, Opera Transatlántica, with a board of directors in Venezuela and another in the UK. The productions we made were miracles and toured many countries. Thanks to Edwin, I went to Venezuela many times and could learn a lot about the culture of the place, which in turn formatively influenced my visual world. That was my first adventure into Latin American magic realism and a genuine revelation – and a dream came true, realised through our new opera company. Edwin was the writer and a partner in the creation which defined the workings of Opera Transatlántica, and gave me a clear vision of the kind of work I wanted to make.

In Opera Transtlántica, we talked a lot about the symbolism of food and memory. Once Edwin brought in a dish of *Moros y Cristianos* (Moors and Christians) – black beans and white rice eaten together – symbolizing the integration of Latin American cultures. Then one day on a long-haul flight with Singapore Airlines to Venezuela, the menu offered a 'Dafina', described as a slow-cooked soup with meat. Dafina in fact is a Sephardi word for *buried* – food for the Sephardi family would be part-cooked on a Friday in a big pan, then buried in the ground covered and wrapped in hay, so that it was ready to eat midday on a Saturday. (See also Mendel 2002.)

Some years later, when our first international community on the European Scenography Centres had departed, Edwin came back to England with a script he had written. He called it *Rondó Adafina: A Soup in Seven Movements*, and it depicted the migration of Jewish refugee communities across centuries. (See also *What is Scenography?*, pp. 184–5.) The story went from 1300 in Morocco to 1999 in Venezuela, charting the expulsion of the Jews from Spain in 1492, many of whom travelled through Iberia, via Amsterdam, Brazil, Curaçao and finally to Coro in Venezuela – the small town where immigrants historically first arrived. The very places in *Rondó Adafina* tell stories. Curaçao has the oldest surviving synagogue in South America dating to 1674, now a concert hall – with sand on the floor. In the town of Coro people settled before they could move further on into Venezuela and its city of Caracas. Until nowadays, the Caracas Museum of Contemporary Art is entirely funded by the descendants of one of these families – who had arrived as poor, dispossessed émigrés and established themselves as one of the richest families in the world.

The aim of our creative process in *Rondó Adafina* was to show how music and food from one country become part of the next and make a theatre journey through space and time. In late August 2000, we began a performance workshop at the Drama Centre in North West London using their round church space. We assembled a great cast, with a choreographer, a composer, a piano and no budget at all. Our aim was to make *a rich theatre out of poor means* – for we never wanted a poor theatre.

The writer and theatre-maker Eleanor Margolies became the wonderful recorder of the process and helped give a sense of the possibilities explored. She listed her documents into eight 'ingredients': tablecloths; the table and the soup pot; verticals and diagonals; speaking tube and suitcase; food on stage; a theatre company prepares a fest; chef or cook; visible and invisible. Having this list, I thought, *What shall we do*? I then remembered my mother's store of unused teatime tablecloths, and put an advert in the local newspaper, the *Ham and High*, inviting local people to bring in unwanted tablecloths. We were overwhelmed! Since we had *no* budget, these cloths became our ammunition. The square cloths proved the most useful scenically: the performers could hold them straight above their heads to create front doors of houses, and then dropping them onto the floor when the soldiers stormed upon them. The round cloths were perfect for improvised skirts and shawls. We were creating what I knew from my childhood –

a theatre of smell, as well as vision and hearing. Flat Venezuelan baskets piled with vegetables or ground spices were placed on the floor by the spectators' feet. There was one basket for each country the story moved to. In each of the places the story moved to, local food was made and local music was played – but always with a presence of the immigrants' own cuisine and song. The smell of the Adafina pot – the pungent aroma of ground spices – was very powerful. The discoveries we made during the workshop that would become our production of *Rondó Adafina* were that our show was both a documentary narrative based on real events and a celebratory pageant with music showing the interaction between the Sephardim and the peoples of the countries they entered. In 2002, Edwin Erminy's *Rondó Adafina* was published and won the First Prize in the prestigious Concurso Literario.

I will never forget the moment when I came to Caracas for our final rehearsals and first performances with Opera Transatlántica. Edwin met me at the airport, and all the walls were covered with posters for our production of *Concierto Barroco*. Then one day we went to the theatre for a rehearsal – only a few days before the opening – and to our astonishment, all the doors were locked and barricaded. No one knew what happened, and we couldn't get in – not even through the staff door at the back. And our first performance was due very soon. Eventually, Edwin learned that the police had come, shut the theatre and cut off our access to the finances: the Teresa Carreño Theatre went bankrupt, but the tickets for our show had already been sold. We had to raise some money quickly and come up with an effective fundraising strategy. We were in the middle of Caracas; looking around, we saw American Express, a Seagram whisky agent, a Venezuelan chocolate exports company Chocolates el Rey and one more international firm. Edwin wrote a script for us to follow: someone would go to the chocolate factory and say: *American Express have been very generous* (which they hadn't, yet) *and could you support our production like American Express?* Another person would go to the whisky agent and say the same about the chocolate company, and so on. It was a story – and it worked. We raised the money. The theatre didn't officially open but through a back door, to which Edwin found a key, we could take our audience in. We led them through the back of the theatre and its corridors to the technical workshops. There we painted twelve old doors red to fit up a provisional stage and stage walls, found a piano and performed there. That night was imprinted on our memory – not only in its actual event but also, metaphorically, as a story of locked doors and ways to open them through the art of making theatre. The London International Festival of Theatre then invited Opera Transatlántica to give five sold-out performances in a warehouse in East London.

We thought we were set on a permanent route for Opera Transatlántica, but sadly politics intervened. Edwin had to leave Caracas at a short notice and take refuge in Port of Spain, Trinidad and Tobago, which had been the home of his father, a well-known art critic. Not deterred, Edwin embarked on a new scenographic journey at the University of Trinidad and Tobago using all the elements of colour and carnival, and sharing his experiences with a group of younger people, with a generosity of spirit that was quite simply amazing. At midnight on New Year's Eve 2018, I received a telephone call from an unknown person in Port of Spain to tell me that there had been a terrible accident. While swimming in the sea – a tradition there to see the New Year in – Edwin had drowned. We had planned to make a new work together, and Edwin had been following closely the development of my work as director/visual creator of the Canadian production of *Charlotte: A Tri-Coloured Play with Music*, always making astute comments, critical and well judged, and more often than not annoyingly correct. I found in my arsenal of treasured textiles a beautiful bright pink sequined cloth from Trinidad with a card from Edwin saying how we would meet in 2019 for the Prague Quadriennal and present our new work. I think often of the brightness of this textile, with sequined sparks of invention flying across the seas like electric currents, and vowed I would aim to continue our work.

Almost everywhere around the world, shops sell bagels. How can that be? As a child, I used to go down to Petticoat Lane in the East End in London – and you can still do that – to a shop run by Pakistani owners who bake bagels in the old, Jewish way. In the old days, the seller would sit outside the shop on a little stool with all the bagels on a little pole. It's simple and convenient: the bagels have a hole in them. Originally, of course, sellers would often not own a shop, and the pole would be their 'emporium' to carry with them wherever they went. With a simple pole they didn't have to pay rent. All they owned or had was just a pole of bagels with holes in them. Once in Caracas I went to the Saturday market, which takes place in a simple car park. To go there on one's own is immensely dangerous. I have never seen such a *mestizo*, mixed group of people in my life! And of course, bagels were sold there too – in the old way. Fundamentally, that's what *Rondó Adafina* was about: how song, music and food get integrated into the host country. Wherever people move, they take with them the food and their cultural memory.

In 2003, a totally unexpected opportunity arrived from dear friends to relocate from South West London to Selsey – 'a little corner of Paradise' by the sea in West Sussex that I knew well and always dreamt about. I used to say to them: *If ever I could live in one of the old railway houses right on the sea I would give up unaffordable London*. I was working in Belgrade in Serbia on a performance piece with students from the Belgrade Academy of Arts, when in the middle of a rehearsal the technician came in with a large portable phone and told me there was a call for me. Who could possibly know where I was? Over the phone, my friend from Selsey told me that the old lady in the railway house opposite them had died, and he and his wife were looking after her affairs as she had no family. He said: *We think it's about time your dream came true and you came here.* I replied, *How can I? I am in Belgrade! And I have a house to sell in London before I can do anything and heaven knows how long that will take.* He replied: *You will have to make a decision now, but we are prepared to buy it for you and you can take as long as you like until you have sold the London house, and repay us after that.* And so I said, *Yes please*, and went back into rehearsal in the old Rex Cinema in Dorćol and thought: *I have just changed my life. . . .* It took me nine months.

Years later, I was in Georgia leading the young theatrical artists' seminar at the Tbilisi Biennal of Scenography, and one of the guest artists from the Ukraine came to me and said: *I don't know if you remember me but years ago I was in your workshop in Belgrade and you came to me and said 'I've just changed my life'. Did you?* I said I did and realised that it was one of the most important changes I have ever made.

When I moved to Selsey, the local historian came to welcome me and presented me with the documents about the house. I was shocked to discover its history. It is constructed out of two old railway carriages and was put down in 1920 by a Polish Jewish émigré called Jacob Berg, who had developed a thriving mantle-makers' business in Brick Lane in the East End 'rag trade' area of London. My father's half-brother, my uncle Louis, also had a small business known as 'Club Row Sports' opposite the Bergs' empire. When I was a small child, my mother used to put me on the train from Newcastle upon Tyne to London under the care of the guard (see ID photo in the Foreword), and in London Uncle Louis would be there to meet me in his old battered car. My childhood memory is of various London 'aunts' asking Uncle Louis how he was and he having one answer: *I'm TERRIBLE.* When they asked him what was the matter, he simply said: *It's the Bergs.* I thought the Bergs were like measles. Uncle Louis gave me a doll I called Bunty to take back home with me. I painted red spots all over her, and when I showed it to my mother, I said, *Bunty's got the Bergs* – and it became a family joke. In those days all clothes manufacturing was done by what was known as 'piece-work' – one was paid so much an arm, so much a leg. It was very hard to survive as a piece-worker, and all the workers were family members. The difference was that the Bergs had major trade contracts, and used to offer local workers a halfpenny more for each piece, so my uncle Louis either had no work, with his own workers to pay, or he had work, but the Bergs had poached all his workers. This was the cut-throat experience of the East End 'rag trade'.

The documents record that Jacob Berg came down to Selsey with a group of friends and walked along the sea, where there were no houses, only fields. He met a farmer and asked him: *Who owns all this land?* And the farmer said: *I do.* Jacob Berg asked him if he wanted to sell it. They exchanged addresses, and after some negotiation, a sale was completed. Jacob Berg was a Freemason, which was very unusual as there was a strict quota on Jews being admitted to Freemason Lodges. In the Lodge was a member who happened to be Head of Redundant Trains at Waterloo Station. In conversation, Jacob Berg told him of his acquisition, and quick as a flash this member suggested that Berg should buy some redundant railway carriages which were in a shed at the back of the station. They formed a business partnership that became known as Park Estates.

When I heard this story, I could not believe I was actually living in the house put down by the man who made my uncle Louis's life such a misery.

When I first moved into this historic railway house, all I saw was a wild overgrown garden full of brambles and nettles, with a huge broken caravan lying on its side, but for the first time in my life I had what is called *liquidity*. My dream was to build a dedicated studio where I could to work every day, having worked all my life in converted bedrooms. And here I have it – my *Arsenal of Dreams* – my store of colours, textures, strings, ribbons, clips, pens and pegs essential to my creative life. I have words, notes, music pinned and pegged everywhere to remind me what to do. And when I am stuck as I frequently am, I can just walk a few steps to the sea and watch the tide coming in and out no matter what happens – and I begin again – the daily fight with the birds as to who owns the raspberry bushes that are rampant in my garden.

My small house in Selsey, West Sussex, is the receptacle of all these memories. The writer Michael Kustow in his book *In Search of Jerusalem* described his last visit to my house in these words:

> Pamela's house is bursting with stories. The stories of the plays she has designed, the stages she has made – [. . .] a cavernous hall in Edinburgh, an open-air auditorium in a Venetian fortress in Thessaloniki. More stories on the Czech and Polish tea-towels [. . .] hung on her walls – embroidered comic strips of a woman in the kitchen cooking, shopping, sweeping [. . .] the faces and figures on posters of her theatre work and the painting and sinuous drawings she has done of characters in her plays and of people observed during rehearsal. [. . .] Drawings like whispers. (Kustow 2009: 132)

Then, as so often in life, events took an unexpected turn. I received an invitation in 2018 to create a new original music theatre piece as part of a festival in Chichester to celebrate Leonard Bernstein at 100. Bernstein had lived for a short time in Chichester and written *The Chichester Psalms* there to be performed by schoolchildren in Chichester Cathedral. I had collaborated previously with the American/UK composer Carl Davis, and we began to dream together. Carl had met Bernstein while living in New York and was wonderfully familiar with his music.

We envisaged several possible scenarios using an ensemble of six singers of different ages, one of whom would also be a pianist and might represent the archetypical 'composer' in his living room in the mid-1950s. We were offered the space at the Chapel on the campus of the University of Chichester. There is a large altarpiece stretching nearly the whole width of the building, with a low wooden rail in the front – like a stage. This gave me an idea. In my studio I had 500 brown paper lunch bags and 56 brown paper carrier bags from Wholefoods Supermarket which I had brought home from Pittsburgh, where I was on a three-month artist in residence stay at Carnegie Mellon University. In my passion for storing things carefully, I found them and stuffed them with old tissue paper and painted tiny windows in black so they appeared to be skyscrapers. I found some old white paper drinking straws to make chimneys and some birds' white feathers for steam coming out of the chimneys. But how to make them look huge? Then my eye caught a big box of coloured paperclips, and I idly twisted one with a small pair of pliers and found I could make tiny paperclip people which made the paper bag skyscrapers look proportionately huge. I stuck them onto cardboard bases (I never throw a good cardboard box away). The festival brochure had a photo of Bernstein conducting the Berlin Philharmonic, and taken out of context it looked exactly as if he were speaking to God. I made 150 copies of the photo, cut them out carefully and fixed each to the top of the paper bag skyscrapers supported by the paper straws – and *là voilà!*: We had the Manhattan landscape. We fixed it to the church altar rail and on tables hidden behind the front row of skyscrapers. Carl and I evolved a programme that used Bernstein's music, texts and lyrics to demonstrate the conflicts in his life: America, New York, the movies, politics, love, God and the finale.

Most people know Bernstein for his *West Side Story* but only few people know the story behind it. When Bernstein started working on the musical, he initially wished to call it the *East Side Story* and write about his parents' emigration from Russia to America and about the ordinary things his family were worried about, such as a washing machine and not knowing how to use it – which was all about his mother. In writing the work, Bernstein got very stuck, depressed and couldn't overcome the block. One day his friend, choreographer Jerome Robbins, came to see him in Brooklyn, where he lived. He invited Lennie – as everyone called him – and suggested to take him out to make him feel better. They went together to a bar overlooking a spot where kids were playing in the playground, with some wire netting behind where a game was taking place. The kids

were shouting and were even being violent – clearly, two competing gangs fighting among themselves. The two friends were morosely sitting over their drinks looking out, until Jerome said to Lennie: *I know what the problem is. It's all too close to you. Why don't you – instead of* East Side Story *– write* West Side Story *and make it about Puerto Ricans? You can use the same songs – but there they all are.* Lennie looked around and thought what a terrible idea that was. Still, he complied but never was entirely happy, unable to get to its essence and was about to give up. Lennie's father was a rabbi, and although Lennie himself wasn't of a religious persuasion – certainly not a practising believer – he went to his father for advice in his hopelessness: he was trying to write the story and still couldn't get it right. His émigré father, the rabbi, said: *Listen, Lennie. Just sing God a simple song.* Lennie started to write *West Side Story* properly – and the rest is history. Bernstein's father's advice to his overanxious son – *Lennie, just sing God a simple song* – became the title of our very successful production.

Another problem came when the last performance of *Sing God a Simple Song* was over: What shall we do with all the painted paper bags? On the last night, as I was taking a final bow, I mentioned my worry to Will Allenby, the singer and pianist, and he said: *Just give it away.* So, I said to the spectators: *If anyone would like to take a piece of the Manhattan landscape home, please feel free to help yourselves.* Within minutes like seagulls descending from the skies, Manhattan was all gone! Until now I meet people who greet me: *Still enjoying my Manhattan landscape!* – and I love the thought that there are bits of our production scattered all over West Sussex and maybe further – for that's what art is all about.

But what is it? A paper bag and a paper clip – and a dream. That's all. In this simple and economic way, ordinary objects turned into theatre or art. It also goes to Lennie's father's words – to sing God a simple song. Without being complicated, it goes right back to the simple things. And in this way, we are released.

I have always loved making 'models'. When during the war our American food parcels arrived, sometime there were flat card boards with eight different colours of 'plasticene' or 'children's modelling clay' – as it is now known. These were strips in narrow lines that could be pulled off separately – and a myriad of colours could be made from rolling small pieces in the palms of two hands until they looked like marbles. Best of all was that they could hold sticks upright, especially old paintbrushes – some long and some small – that my architect uncle used to give me when he had worn out the bristles. I loved these because they still had bits of bright colour, and the hairy tops suggested faces in the sky. I made houses from sticks and paintbrushes and sometimes – if I found long paintbrushes – I could make big doorways that I pretended led to palaces in the sky. My grandfather in 'the old country' in Belorussian Minsk was a cabinetmaker, and though he was in poor health by the time I knew him, he always had a penknife in his pocket and a bit of wood – and he carved little figures to go through my doorways, though they never stood up.

In my studio today, people marvel at my organization – as I have boxes and boxes of ammunition for making models and a huge collection of old paintbrushes, corks, string, pins, glue, knives and corrugated papers from chocolate boxes – all immensely useful for 1:25-scale models. When I make a model for a production, it's much more than a technical exercise. It has texture, colour and form, and *describes the space* that the scale figures (representing the actors) I make from thin wires, plasticene, tissue paper and paint will occupy. These maquettes go hand in hand with the *thinking drawings*, so everyone can see how the proposal might work. I can always see potential in materials that others throw away. Old habits never die!

One unrealised dream – one of the many that got rejected and refused – started with a mistake. While I was working on a commissioned project, I was also planting some seeds in small cardboard pots in my garden. I accidentally made a hole in the pot and was dismayed. But as I was thinking how to do the project, instead of throwing the pot away, I came back into my studio and cut a small window in the pot and from a staple made a little handle – and suddenly the entire idea came to me. I used another five pots, cut out windows in them and placed them bottom-up in a hexagon shape with the windows facing out. And there stood not only a circle of tiny mansions that could become performance spaces but their roofs created a platform up there, as it were in heaven. Breughel's painting *The Tower of Babel* inspired me – and here stood its base. Ever since I was fifteen and was expelled from school, I dreamed that one day I could make a music theatre piece about Breughel's painting, thinking of Brecht: *In the dark times, will there also be singing?*

Inside Breughel's tower shines a dark red glow and I wondered how to make it. When I was an art student in Birmingham in the mid-1950s, we were encouraged to get experience in other departments too. I went into the textile department and tried my hand at silk screen printing. As a student, I only did it on cheap brown paper rather than on actual silk – and now, as I was thinking of the Tower of Babel, I wished I had a roll of brown paper like that to use. And I reached under my working desk, and there it was! So, I was able to make the silk screen prints on paper panels – a skill I had learned back in Birmingham. It remains an unexplained miracle how that roll of brown paper could be there, waiting for me. And it came in handy to create the red glow, and I attached it to corrugated cardboard (itself a leftover from an online delivery packing) that I mounted on a structure of skewers to create the tall walls of the tower.

The painter Max Birne had died shortly before. He was a dear friend of mine and I helped him in the last months of his life when he was unable to go out shopping. I went to see him almost every afternoon and we talked about painting and painters. Although he couldn't see any more, he still continued painting. Of course, his work was different, almost pointillist, as he could not discern lines but he could just about feel colours. Max and I used to exchange brushes. So, when he died, I thought, *Max is in the sky*, and Breughel's tower has a door as if it were a gateway to heaven – so, in my speculative model I used two of Max's thin, long brushes as posts to a doorway leading to heaven. When an acrylics manufacturer from London came to visit me and saw the model, I asked him for a transparent box to preserve this dream of mine. I told him the story behind it, and he saw the paintbrushes – and he loved the idea so much that he refused to take any payment for the acrylic box he made for it.

It's the paintbrushes that please me most: they are not only a memory but also a monument to Max. When I spoke to him shortly before his death, I asked him if there was something he wished for in his life that he hasn't had. He said, *Yes. I want an exhibition in a place where no one has ever had one.* A few hours later he died, and I was the last person he spoke to. On the anniversary of his death, we arranged a small exhibition with friends to whom Max had given joy through his art.

That mistake of making hole in a pea pot – was it a disaster, or was it an opportunity?

In my early years in Newcastle on Tyne, the acrid smell of sulphur was always in the air, for Newcastle was famous for its coal mines. A horse and cart came down our street with bags of coal to stoke our fires, and many people including my grandfather suffered from chest complaints. I used to sit on the stairs each morning and watch the early morning ritual of saving the ashes from the day before and relighting the new day's fire. My grandfather kneeling on the floor carefully scraping the previous day's ashes onto a large piece of newspaper resting on the stone hearth. New coals were placed into the grate and the ashes scattered among them. Then the newspaper was held up in front of the fireplace to prevent any air from coming in, matches were put between the fresh coals and the ashes, and my grandfather had to blow his own air into the bottom of the grate, while my grandmother shouted at him in Yiddish. Eventually after some time, the coals began to light, the newspaper was put onto the fire and my poor grandfather flopped exhausted into his old leather armchair. They did not know that bellows existed for this procedure. Out of the ashes came fire, and the daily cooking could begin.

That memory of my grandparents over the old ashes returned to me and became part of our *Charlotte: A Tri-Coloured Play with Music*. When Charlotte Salomon drew her previous life from memory, she looked at it and thought: *Is this my life? or is it theatre?* Then sensing the end was coming, she wrapped all her drawings with their tracing paper titles overlaid into a brown paper parcel and left them in the care of the local doctor, writing on the package, *Take good care of these. It is my whole life.* In 1943, she and her newly wedded husband were taken to Auschwitz concentration camp and murdered in the gas ovens. In my production, the final scene shows her standing alone on the stage with all the characters in her life appearing as ghosts to Aleš Březina's music. Charlotte holds out her book to the audience and says: *Out of the ashes . . .* – and the lights go out. I am very proud of that moment and the fact that her work is well known through the many books, theatre productions, films, operas as well as our production. They all bear a testament to the power of art and making theatre, and they also bring together my own personal memories from early days in my grandparents' house and the daily ritual of saving the ashes of the day before.

Making theatre is always about giving audiences a chance to experience the unexpected. Sometimes using the internet makes us complacent and reduces our searches to what we immediately want. But there is another way. One is to make foyer exhibitions so that people have to walk through, before they enter the auditorium. In this way, one can also pass knowledge. Probably all of us who have had some life experience and therefore knowledge, in whatever our field is, have to rethink how we provide a more interesting alternative than simply saying: *Well, you can look it up on the web*. Sometimes, even the theatres where we are performing have no perception or understanding why this could be important – and that's a very hard situation for artists. We have to accept that some people are unwilling to see and hear, and won't understand the value before they see it.

One has to learn how to be curious about things that we didn't even know about. How do we make space for the entirely unknown? How do we find the tributaries to the river? Sailing down the stream is straightforward but where are the tributaries that feed into it? The most rewarding moments in my own creative life are the revelations of the stories behind the story of the text. I am always thinking when I make a piece of theatre that we should let our eyes see what our ears can't hear, and vice versa. When making the visual environment, it is possible to add to a person's comprehension by finding its unique difference.

A
TRI-COLOURED
WORLD

As a child in the Second World War, I loved drawing with colours. I did not have wooden pencils or even know of their existence. I had chalks and wax crayons with paper coverings that had to be carefully peeled off before one could use them. With the wax crayons, I drew as everyone did – on cardboard boxes, on brown paper carrier bags, on used large envelopes – for plastics were yet to come into our lives. With the wax crayons, I used to draw on the concrete wall of our outside lavatory. It was perfectly ordinary, just as cutting up newspapers into squares, punching a hole through a corner, threading them onto string and putting them on the hook in the lavatory for toilet paper was. My 'masterpiece' on the wall was a circus with clowns – I had never seen a circus except in a book – and that drawing stayed there for many years protected from the rain. My mother said that if I wanted to be an artist, I had to have a beret – and she knitted an artist's beret for me out of scraps of wool that were left over from a pullover she had unwound with me holding the wool in two small hands. I loved that hat and wore it when I was 'being an artist'. I was always busy – sitting on the sofa shaking half-pint bottles of milk until they became solid enough to be put in a net over the sink – to become either butter or cream cheese. This was the world we all lived in and in some ways I never left.

Wax crayons work well on cardboard boxes. The colours are strong and bold, which for children is really important and basic. The first mark a child makes has to give them joy, so that they get excited and want to continue and progress in mark-making without fear of 'going wrong' and endlessly 'rubbing out' – which is the definition of pencil drawing. As someone who is passionate about teaching drawing, my practice is to encourage students to learn to *look* instead of learning to *draw*, which is the result of looking. I show children and young people how to 'Take a line for a walk' through the paintings of Paul Klee. The test is to fill a blank paper without taking the crayon or pencil off the surface. I usually do it to music, and we do get some wonderful results. When our monthly cardboard boxes arrived from Cousin Jackie in America, my mother always asked me to draw a picture with my wax crayons to include in her letter of thanks. Then something very exciting happened, for one day there was a special parcel in the box for me, and when I opened it – I think I was four and a half years old – it was a box of oil pastels. Cousin Jackie always included something special for

me – sometimes plasticene, sometimes chalks – and now oil pastels. We had never seen such things. I realised that I could draw not just on paper but also on the outside wall – and the rain couldn't wash it off! Jackie had written a note saying I should take red, yellow and blue, and see how many colours I could make out of just these three colours – draw round a saucer to make a big circle and colour it in red. Then take each of the other two colours, blue and yellow, and colour on top of the red and see how many different colours appear. How exciting a suggestion that was! I couldn't mix colours with chalks, but now the arsenal of my art expanded immensely. When we opened the box of pastels, we saw that they were arranged exactly like the colours of a rainbow. Unlike the hard crayons my mother bought from a relative's grocery corner shop down the road, these American oil pastels were soft and pliable. My mother and I coloured the whole plain cardboard box, and it became a kennel for my beloved toy dog.

Life went on. The war ended, my father came back and we moved to Birmingham, and I eventually became an art student at Birmingham College of Art. In 1958, my last year there, through a personal contact with the great artist and painter John Piper (1903–92) – whose works I still revere – I was asked if I would go to Aldeburgh in Suffolk to help the English Opera Group present a new community opera called *Noye's Fludde*. It was explained to me that sleeping accommodation would be a sleeping bag on the floor in a nearby school in Orford along with other 'volunteers'. I agreed and duly sat in the back of someone's car, as we drove across England. Being a very literal young person, I did not realise Suffolk was by the sea. The rehearsals with Benjamin Britten, Peter Pears and the chamber ensemble were thrilling and established in my arsenal a lifelong love of his music. But it was sharply pointed out to me that I was not there for the music but to paint a large rainbow on a double bed sheet that was hanging from a balcony in the village hall. I went to see it, and there were some tall stepladders, a groundsheet on the floor and a trestle table with empty jam jars. *Where are the paints and brushes?* I asked timidly – it suddenly dawned on me that I was supposed to have come fully equipped to do the (unpaid) job. The production manager heaved a heavy sigh and said he would see what he could do, gave me a stick, some charcoal and tape and suggested that I should start marking out the seven arcs of rainbow. It is extremely difficult to draw from

a height on a soft cloth but warily I had a go. After some time, an elderly lady came, carrying a large bottle of blackcurrant juice Ribena, a large used toothbrush and a jug of water. She asked me if this would do for the red of the rainbow. I was horrified but had no alternative but to try, remembering fondly my American oil pastels. I poured some Ribena into a jam jar, dipped the toothbrush in, climbed the ladder and aimed for a curve. A large red drip fell the length of the sheet – and I thought this is not the promise God made to Noah. Eventually, after much debate someone went to Aldeburgh and bought some jars of paints. The lady washed the Ribena off the sheet. The sheet was then laid on the floor, and a gift from local residents of old paintbrushes was produced. It was a miracle that I finally made that rainbow. It was only much later that I realised what a privilege it was to have been in the company of those great people, and especially Imogen Holst (1907–84, daughter of composer Gustav Holst), who took me under her wing. I later found out what a significant figure in twentieth-century British music she was, but at the time she was like a mother to me. She took me to see another Britten piece in Aldeburgh called *The Little Sweep*, and I saw the magic of a horse and coach made from a borrowed rocking horse, two small chairs behind and two open umbrellas held by singers representing the wheels of the chariot. The impact of this image – a momentary composition that could be immediately dissolved – was magical and impressed itself on my memory. It was that which I later called *making a rich theatre out of little means*.

In 1959 I got married, and we moved to London so I could attend the postgraduate course at the Slade School of Fine Art. I completed the course in 1962 and started a small theatre business with two friends. Fate, however, had other ideas. I became ill. At first seemingly not serious, then getting worse and worse with many hospitalizations. Eventually I was diagnosed with a form of ovarian cancer, and at the age of twenty-seven underwent a hysterectomy. I had to take some time out to convalesce. John Crockett (1918–84), a good friend, was an accomplished theatre and television film director. In 1962, he saw some of my drawings in an exhibition and invited me to design the costumes for his production for IKON Theatre Company of Dostoevsky's *The Idiot*. IKON had taken a residency at the Lyric Theatre Hammersmith, originally a music hall, later rebuilt by the theatre architect Frank Matcham (1854–1920), and renovated in 1979. This new production of *The Idiot* presented young acting talent, many of whom became the great names of British theatre. This was my first major commission, and it all happened simply because I did some drawings that were shown in a small exhibition.

John had previously created a travelling theatre company known as Compass Theatre presenting what they called 'Plays without Theatres' throughout England. He lived with his family of six children in the country. As his work was now to be based in London, he suggested we exchanged for a short period our London flat for his eight-seater British-drive camper van, and my husband and I set off for Bern in Switzerland where relatives were ready to welcome us.

We drove peacefully through Europe, stopping at a few monuments, and finally we were on the autobahn from Basel to Bern. On the opposite side of the road we saw a large lorry, with a transporter at the back carrying ballast used to make roads. Everything was quiet, peaceful and sunny. Suddenly there was an enormous bang like an explosion, and to our horror we saw that this large trailer had broken away from the lorry and crashed through the central road barrier. My husband tried to lessen the impact of the inevitable collision by crashing the Volkswagen into a concrete post on the side of the road. He was able to get out, but I was at ninety degrees to the trailer which then upturned over the Volkswagen and completely buried me. The lorry driver drove on and then looked in his mirror and wondered why all the traffic behind him stopped. Suddenly he realised that his trailer was missing, and at the next slip road he turned around and presented himself to the Swiss police. By that time, police and ambulances were all around. I was conscious the whole time and was very carefully dug out, and taken by ambulance to the nearest hospital – Tiefenau in Bern. By a miracle, I had not moved, though the X-rays revealed I had broken the second vertebra in my spine. It was only a hair's breadth that the break did not touch the spinal cord; otherwise I would have been paralysed. They cleaned me up as much as possible and made a plaster cast for me, so that I could not move, and put me in traction and on a life support machine. The irony was that the Swiss police classified the accident as 'An Act of God', since all Swiss vehicles are required by law to undergo rigorous and frequent safety checks, and the lorry had met all the necessary criteria. In turn, we very quickly received charges for importing a vehicle illegally even though John's camper was a complete write-off, and of course for this we were not insured. Our parents flew over to Bern but I was not aware of anything – and finally my husband returned to London to await events.

It was here in the Tiefenau hospital after three weeks that I regained my life entirely, due to a meeting with the near-blind physiotherapist Lily Marbach – who shouted at me in perfect English and said: *YOU ARE NOT ILL! YOU HAVE JUST HAD AN ACCIDENT. THAT IS ALL!* – and she removed the life support machine. I did not die.

The next day I faintly heard a huge commotion outside my room. Lily had some hospital workers wheel in a huge drawing board not unlike the one my uncle Henry used for his architectural perspectives. They placed it so that it was either side of my bed – it was exactly the image of me as a little girl looking at the drawing board. Then she came with some large gardening canes, with a crayon attached to each end – red, yellow and blue – and in a commanding voice instructed me to draw my life in a hospital bed. She also supplied me with a pair of ninety-degree prismatic glasses so I could see who was coming through the door without having to turn, and she made me record my days by drawing everything – however horrific it was. After a number of weeks – and I truly can't remember how long – they took the plaster cast off me: there were mushrooms growing out of my head because all the dirt from the road had been left inside the cast – I still have a drawing of it. I had temporarily lost the use of my left arm, but fortunately I am right-handed, and on the large drawing pad attached to the board I began 'drawing for my life' and creating another tri-coloured world. My accident was huge news, and Swiss people started sending gifts and cards, and this went on for the half year I was there. It was summer when we left England and winter when I was able to get out of my cast and start with Lily's help to move again, and people sent donations of winter clothes. Lily and my husband and I became great friends, and later she came to visit us several times. She even drew a portrait of me with the face of death as a shadow behind me. She saved my life.

I was in hospital for six months, and this gave me the time to think about what I was really doing with my life – if I had a life that I would go back to. When I was at the Slade School of Fine Art, there were two people I was friendly with – Judith Wood, who was a painter, and Jenny Levy, who had a substantial track record of making jewellery for opera houses and other institutions. Together we set up a small theatre jewellery and prop-making business. We called ourselves Theatre Arts and used one of the rooms in our Paddington Street flat as a workroom. Gradually, we started to get commissions, and the big one was from Franco Zeffirelli (1923–2019) to make five huge carnival horses for performers to wear for his opera production at the Royal Albert Hall. The problem of course was how to get the five horses there. We soon realised that the police wouldn't let us take any of the main roads, and while the production manager tried to figure out the transport, Jenny, Judy, myself and two assistants – one of whom was Robin Phillips (1940–2015), who later became the director of Stratford Ontario and Chichester Festival Theatre – just got into the carnival horses and walked them through the back streets down to the Royal Albert Hall. But that whole escapade made me think: *Why am I doing this? Do I want to carry on making horses and running through Marble Arch in a horse outfit? – I don't think I do.* When I came home from this event, I was unsure – and then we went to Switzerland, and the car accident happened. At that point, I realised that when I come back from Switzerland, I could not go on as I was before and I would not.

That was the true beginning of my work – initially as a designer and later as a director-scenographer. It all came down to Lily Marbach saying, *You're not ill. You just had an accident*, going out into the hospital garden, putting a crayon on the end of a stick and saying, *Draw* – and I was drawing for my life. That was a seminal moment for me – one could say, *Out of darkness comes light*.

Back in London, I slowly began to rebuild my life, remembering a saying of my grandfather's, relating to their forced escape from their former home in Minsk: *Crisis? What crisis? It's an opportunity! –* and I determined to change my way of working however long it took, and to aim to make work that really mattered to me. Our Theatre Arts business had already ceased to be, and I had to walk through that open door into a new world. I continued needing medical treatment and was fortunate to be assigned to a visionary orthopaedic surgeon. He not only manipulated me, but listened to me, and advised me to read William Blake's *Songs of Innocence and Experience*. In a Charing Cross Road bookshop, I found this tiny book, handwritten (originally) in three colours with little drawings, and discovered that Blake was a true interdisciplinary artist – poet, painter and printmaker. I devoured the poems like someone dying of thirst in the desert, and then by chance in Hampstead I met the poet Adrian Mitchell (1932–2008), and we had a coffee. I told him about my 'discovery', and he said languidly that he knew all about Blake because he was developing a small theatre piece at the National Theatre called *Tyger* based on Blake's life, with the jazz composer Mike Westbrook, Kate Westbrook and Michael Kustow – and I could come along if I wished. And I did take the opportunity without thinking of being paid for it, and it did me far more good than any medical interventions. I began to focus on my dreams while in my innocence getting as much experience as I could – and I still had my knitted artist's beret.

I was twenty-four and not long graduated from the Theatre Department of the Slade School of Art, wondering where destiny would take me. I had got to know Ralph Koltai, who was then thirty-nine, through our shared familial roots. He told me how he had met the singer Lotte Lenya in Brown's Hotel, entertained her at tea and acquired the rights to present his version of the Brecht-Weill singspiel *The Rise and Fall of the City of Mahagonny*. In 1963, Ralph had managed to persuade the director Michael Geliot to present this at Sadler's Wells Theatre. This was a very important year artistically and personally for Koltai, and it was then that one of his philosophical sayings evolved: *I give directors what they want before they know they want it.* The moment when a real lorry drove onto the stage caused the entire audience to gasp. The sides of the lorry opened up to reveal a space that could be a brothel and an execution chamber, enhanced by projections we had never seen. It was unforgettable. The legacy of this event exists in one remarkable sketchbook in which Ralph painted with a thick watercolour brush and Indian ink the entire production step by step – with stage instructions typed on an old-fashioned typewriter stuck below each picture. This sketchbook is unlike anything Ralph had ever done or ever did again and turning its now-delicate pages, stored carefully in his studio in France, it is as fresh and innovative today as it was on that day in 1963.

Those American oil pastels I received during the war from Cousin Jackie gave me an everlasting search for colours and materials that would express the subject, and I could fall in love with. When in 2015 I was commissioned to direct and create the visual world of *Carmen* for the National Opera of Ljubljana, Slovenia, I was completely stuck. I could not find the medium. To try and clear my head, I went for a walk by the sea where I now live. I often pick up stones to put in my garden from the shingle on the beach, and I saw one that attracted me. I picked it up. When I returned to the studio and felt it, I saw it was not a stone but a dirty car-cleaning chamois leather cloth that had been thrown away and hardened by the wind and sea. I flattened it in warm water, and by chance saw a bottle of dark-brown mineral pitch a friend had sent me from Barcelona. It was called *Betún de Judea* (Jew's blood). I put a brush on the chamois leather and made a mark – and fell in love with it. The next day I was driving to the supermarket, and I passed a large cycle and car accessory store. Outside was a big notice saying CHAMOIS LEATHER CLOTHS 3 FOR 2! I went in and bought the lot. When I got home, I opened the packets and saw that each one was a different shape, and I realised I could make compositions of characters responding to the shape of the cloth. And thus *Carmen* began. My oil pastels synchronized with the dark-brown mineral pitch lines, and the soft leather cloths could just roll up without taking up much room. Perfect *joy*!

Artistic creation and the life of an artist are hard. One has to build faith in oneself, cope with rejection and misunderstanding, and survive loneliness. Doubting oneself, walking hand in hand with fear and always trying – all this is central to artistic creation.

When I was a child, I thought it was my mission in life to be in conflict with people and to stand my ground. Gradually I learned that there is nothing to be gained from getting into conflict with others and made a resolution to always try to win cleverly by finding an alternative route. Many people that I know don't understand what I do and think I am just mad. This perhaps comes from being an artist – always dreaming of making something beautiful, of catching a soul and handing it to a performer. I often feel like an outsider – I come from somewhere, and I belong nowhere. I make theatre by realizing dreams from around the world, even if they aren't immediately understood.

One of the watershed moments in my life happened to me several years ago. I am very fond of Chekhov, and have done a number of his plays. I love the balance of the words and the plays as such. One day I got a phone call from the National Theatre in London, offering me to design their new production of *Uncle Vanya*. I had done *Uncle Vanya* twice, and I thought to myself: *How many times can a girl draw a pair of black button boots? I have done that and I don't want to do it again.* So, I thanked them kindly for asking me, apologized and explained that I had done it twice. They were deeply offended – not because I said *I'm sorry but I am doing a musical in New York*, but because I said it as it was.

That incident made me think: if I don't want to do *Uncle Vanya* again, I need to start dreaming about the work that I would like to make myself. That was a turning point for me – the moment when my present state of work took off, but also a moment of reflection of what I wanted to achieve within my remaining years. I wanted to tell stories about the world I knew and how those stories and memories affected our lives. I am interested in what happens to people when political events disrupt their lives, in dislocation and relocation, and I've looked for subjects that illuminate that theme.

This resolution has led on to several of my productions – from the chamber opera *The Marriage*, written by Czech composer Bohuslav Martinů (1890–1959) when he was a penniless exile in New York, to *The Ballad of the Cosmo Café*, which had an important link to my own life. The story is not only about a younger me going into a café, but there are moments that carry much more meaning. One of the songs that Philip Glassborow wrote for *The Ballad*, 'Questions, Always Questions', portrays my family for instance. My family would always speak in questions, and I never knew why that was. I grew up in an environment believing that no one was really expected to understand one another because I lived in a mélange of languages. When, as a student, I happened to go into the Cosmo Café – where everybody spoke a different language or at least in an accent – I felt I was at home. The place was much more than a café. Many writers have written about their fascination that not only did everyone know each other in the Cosmo but they also *misunderstood* everybody else. That is a world I knew and that's what I dreamed of showing in the production. Bringing together my own life and my art of making theatre was the realization of my dream. In it I found the expression of the resolution I had made all those years before.

Many years ago, I went to Toledo and was profoundly moved. During the Spanish Inquisition and after the expulsion of Moors and Jews from Spain, Toledo was the one place where they could go. It has always been a mixture of people from different faiths and different cultures. One day, a young man walked from Crete to Toledo and stood on the bridge looking at the city with its multiple architecture, and he drew *The Toledo Panorama*. The young man became known as El Greco (The Greek, 1541–1614) and became the painter of Toledo. The dramatist and poet Federico García Lorca, the filmmaker Luis Buñuel and the painter Pablo Picasso were among the many who were inspired by El Greco's story and whom Toledo has filled with wonder. It was my dream to tell Toledo's story, and El Greco's painting became the inspiration behind my own performance piece called simply *The Toledo Panorama*. It is not only about Toledo and El Greco but also in a way my personal story. I have been dreaming of telling it for some thirty years.

As an artist I am crossing the borderline between making theatre visually and making it in actuality. That crossing of the borderline often confuses people and requires having faith in one's own art and be ready for the confusion and lack of understanding. I often find that it is organizers and producers who may be afraid – knowing all the financial and other risks. Naturally, building faith in oneself is never just about the artist – one cannot build it if people are afraid of interacting with the work. One can hardly build faith in oneself without doing the work. Strangely, now that I am unable to go to all the places around the world, I cannot be there to interpret or explain it. This is a very different scenario: the work has to speak for itself and for me too. But it's the work that one needs to do first – without it the conversation can't even start.

Sometimes students ask me what is success and what is failure. They want to be successful, and they are told different things about what that means. And of course they are afraid of failure. For me, failure is not being true to yourself. If you can be true to yourself, you've succeeded. There is one important step to take: as artists we have to be able to move from subjectivity to objectivity. One needs to ask oneself: *Have I made that transition?* This may sound like coming from a psychologist but that's not how I mean it. The point is to make the artwork and make it available to others – from a dream to its realization. That transition is part of the critical debate over making art.

Sometimes one has to acknowledge that we cannot achieve everything just on our own – and I am the living example of that. I don't consider myself very good at writing but if I can work with someone collaboratively, I can find a way of expressing in words what I would do in visual art. So, one also needs to let people into one's world and share that world. That's important for thriving. In the story of *The Unicorn and Joe* – a production we are working on with Philip Glassborow – when Joe finds his third goldfish dead, Kandinsky gives him a mint and tells him to get his mind off it. He explains to him that fishes don't thrive in a bowl, but Joe doesn't know what thriving means. When he then finds the unicorn he has been looking for (which isn't a unicorn but a one-horned kid), he asks the Unicorn Man: *Does it thrive?* While this is just a small word spoken by a child, it has much bigger connotations.

I try to say to students: *Don't come into this business if you can't take rejection, because it will upset you.* Rejection becomes part of the artist's life. Every day in the morning when I come to work in the studio, I say to myself: *Today I walk hand in hand again with fear, and with fear comes rejection.* To use a musical metaphor: we succeed only by acknowledging, as a singer does, that we can come from bottom A to top A; by realizing that we can be at the bottom, but that we can get to somewhere in the middle, if not to the top of the scale that we set ourselves. In *The Unicorn and Joe*, when Joe asks Kandinsky what thriving is, and if he himself thrives, Kandinsky replies, *For me, Joe, it's enough. I survive. That's all I'm asking.*

When we were discussing our production of *The Unicorn and Joe* with Philip Glassborow, this book – *The Art of Making Theatre: An Arsenal of Dreams in 12 Scenes* – was very much in my mind. This is the song Philip wrote:

DREAM BIG DREAMS

Dream big dreams
And plan big plans,
But who knows what the future may hold?
If you plan big plans
And dream big dreams,
Then your dreams may turn into gold.
What is life, but dreams?
Working and loving and dreaming.
They give life its meaning.
That's always what you find
When you keep a dream in mind.
So take your aim
And stake your claim –
Fortune always favours the bold.
And if you dream big dreams
And plan big plans,
Then you'll never ever grow old.

This was the result of Philip and I talking about dreams. Oddly, the show is also about similar things like this book – all the setbacks we are experiencing, the delays, the arguments and everything. In some way, this is what Lily Marbach said to me in hospital in Switzerland: *You're not ill. You just had an accident.* At that point, I had truly reached the bottom, and I wasn't given any life expectancy at all. And even if I had survived, everyone expected that I would be a paraplegic in a wheelchair. It is not necessarily easy, but if one has the vision, one can make the plan and perhaps achieve it.

I believe there are two aspects to success: how you see what you do, and how other people receive what you do – and these may not be the same things. It has happened to me many times that what I thought myself as hugely successful, other people thought was bad. I believe that one shouldn't be obstinate but courageous, for measuring success is a complicated matter. *The Ballad of the Cosmo Café* could serve as an example: a small production that became more than the sum of its parts. There I would measure the success not necessarily by the public acclaim but by the number of phone calls or letter and others that people sent because were moved by the production and how it spoke for a lot of them. One of the lines of the show is, *There's an elephant in the room: So many things that can't be spoken* – but *Cosmo* succeeded in speaking it for those who came to see it, which relieved many people of the necessity of trying to find those words.

For many people, the measure of success is different. They may go and have a lovely evening out watching a musical show. They are given pleasure, enjoyment and excitement. But it's transient, and I personally am profoundly interested in the other way – perhaps in something that's more subversive. For me, success is whether I can create something – with paint, with paper, with card, whatever it is. How do I do that? How do I make an image, a maquette or something I can fall in love with? And frankly, if I am not in love with it, I can't do it. If I succeed, then other people can fall in love with it too, even if they say they are not brave enough to do it themselves. So, in the first instance success is very lonely: it's not anyone else but me. And I always tell myself: Remember, like love, success does not always last. It's a fickle partner, and you always have to reinvent it. On a very material level, that's why I have to look for different materials in order to find it again.

There is also another way of thinking of success. In my studio, I have the poster of *Master and Margarita* from the great

Russian director Yuri Lyubimov (1917–2014), who was a master of reinvention. He was working at the Taganka Theatre on a production of Tchaikovsky's opera *The Queen of Spades*, and the government tried to stop him and put him into prison for doing this allegedly dangerous and subversive production. At the time, I was with the Théâtre National Populaire, and Roger Planchon organized an international initiative. Because he himself could not travel, he sent me to Moscow to put my handprint on the wall and sign my name in support of Lyubimov. Finally, Lyubimov did not go to prison, through our united intervention – and that's another form of success: the strength of artists coming together in solidarity. One of the reasons why Prague Quadrennial is so important is because it offers a structure that enables such international artistic solidarity to happen. Artists get to know one another and appreciate their art despite all the differences – and whenever artists need help, there is a support system. It may appear that this is less of an issue today but only seemingly so – if we think of Latin America, Catalonia, Ukraine or other places. There still is oppression, tyranny and the denial of freedom.

Every artist walks hand in hand with fear. I happened to be at a private view in a small museum in Paris that collects the works Picasso donated in lieu of taxes to the French nation. An American woman came from one of the rooms, saw Picasso standing there and said: *Mr Picasso!* Picasso bowed low and said, *Madame?* The woman continued, *Mr Picasso, this work is no better than that of a child!* Picasso bowed low again and said: *Thank you so much, madame, this is what I have been trying to achieve all my life.* That has stuck with me as a metaphor for the vulnerable creativity and uncertainty we all have as artists. When he takes the handles from a bicycle and sees the horns of a bull in them – that's having faith in oneself and that's very important. It's good to be knowledgeable but it's also good to preserve the curiosity of a child.

Composing a picture derives from the power of opposites, and Picasso in particular was masterful at this: his *Guernica* is built on opposites if one looks closely enough. Looking at the composition and its contrasts tells an important story: here is a man with no money, and, as it happens, he is in the space on a raised stage – and here is a woman with all the money but she is lower down, and yet occupies a bigger space. The two are completely opposite to one another. It's remarkable how these principles are ingrained in one's head. This is what one learns and then how one applies it, often entirely intuitively. And combined with this is the world of multiplicity of languages: the old man and the young man – representatives of two completely different generations; and then the old woman, but she has absolutely nothing to do with the old man – and one can see very clearly the difference in status – all thanks to the power of opposites and the ability to see them with children's eyes.

Technique and skills themselves can become a trap and, for me at least, real creativity can only come when I am able to get myself into a state of being – what I call – as naked as a newborn baby. I have to put aside everything I know and start from nothing. Just because I have made the drawings for *Carmen* on chamois leather doesn't mean that that's my technique and that I know how to do that. Being curious and open to discovery is crucial. It may happen that I come across something unexpected, or I make a mark – and that sets me off. I equate it to composing music: how one finds in composing the musical key in which to write the piece. One doesn't know it but only feels it in advance. My composer friend Aleš Březina speaks about feeling the sound, and he feels the musical key for his composition in advance. I know myself that I am full of fear. I used to be very frightened as an artist – now I am less so but still fearful because I never know how to make the first mark on a piece of paper.

So, for example, when I was starting to work on *The Unicorn and Joe*, I had no idea how to go about it, how to make the drawings: *What do I want from them? How are other people going to read them?* And I thought: *I can't, I just can't do it.* But then I remembered that I always meant to clear out the second drawer of my plan chest, which is full of rubbish. There I came across an unopened packet of imperial sheets of blotting paper (roughly the size of A1). I looked at a sheet and thought: I wonder if I could cut it into eight pieces – because I knew I had to do sixteen drawings. And then I thought – if I had a crayon that is like an aquarell, I could use it sometimes with water and sometimes dry. So, I tried a bit – and I fell in love with it. That set me off, and the adventure of creation started. If I knew what I was going to do before I did it, I wouldn't be able to do it. The important thing is that I have to go back to babyhood, to just being born, and think: I am ready to try and set out on an adventure, no matter where it's going.

The skill is actually not in the technique but in one's ability to have a critical debate with oneself – to know that when you have done something, that it is right or not for your work. Don't draw with pencil and then rub it out. You've got to just do it directly onto the material – either you can do it, or you can't. And finding the love for the material you are working with becomes a crucial point of departure for one's creative adventures.

I made the sixteen drawings for *The Unicorn and Joe*, and I sent them to the cast. They loved them and got confidence from them because they could see that they were dealing with something that is real. One of the actors, Jack Klaff, saw the sketch of his character and said to me: *It's brilliant because all you need is a tape measure, and you are a tailor.* That detail made the dream clear to him – it's the joy of small things and this is how it happens. When one works in theatre, one may think that one is working for oneself, but that's not really true because we are always giving it away. In my position as both a visual creator and what people call the director, I have to give actors the confidence in knowing what they're doing.

It all started with a bit of blotting paper and the wax aquarell, and with playing how I could get different textures with it. When I eventually sent them out to people, their reaction amazed me. That is to say, the technique in this kind of theatrical work is a means to an end. However, going back to the words of Roger Planchon, if you don't like what you have done, then stop it and do something else. When I made the drawings for *The Unicorn and Joe*, I needed to create the environment to show what I wanted to say in words but couldn't. I created a bigger drawing and asked my printer to reduce it, cut out individual images and created perspectives. In other words, the drawings were just the beginning, and it was only in working with them that I could invent a technique using printing to create the environment – the world of the play.

It's a curious thing but I am convinced that coming to make art as naked as a newborn baby is what creativity is about. A baby knows nothing but discovers something, and that something creates the arsenal of what that child might do.

I often feel lonely and isolated but that probably goes with being an artist. One has to depend on oneself – having only yourself to talk to. Although I have been involved with many projects where artists exchanged ideas and reworked them, the critical debate is always with oneself. One has to accept that. Aleš Březina once described it like getting into a boat and going on a long journey over the seas without knowing where the boat is going to take you. It's a very different experience – one is alone, trying to feel it and think it. Even if we change the work later on, when we give it away to others, one has to create it first. And that is a lonely road – and sometimes it's very hard.

Joan J. Guillèn, the founder of the Catalan theatre company La Fura dels Baus (The Rats of the Sewer), once said to me: *An artist has to be prepared to be one of la fura dels baus.* Being a rat underneath is how I would describe subversion. I think that most creative artists probably work on two different levels. One is the level of doing the proper thing – sometimes even against what one's instincts are – but as Ibsen would have said: *To thyself alone be true.* That line from *Peer Gynt* has always inspired me, and the production of 1967 that I designed was one of the most important works of my young life at the Birmingham Repertory Theatre (with Brian Cox as Peer) – at a moment when I stopped being the maker of dead leaves. The dilemma – and often my dilemma – is not just how to do the right thing for the theatre company but how to tell the true story. And that's the other level. How do I make a compromise that isn't a compromise but people think it is? This is not about wanting to be famous, to be on television or being a popular artist doing graffiti on a wall – which is a sort of subversion that has become completely commercialized. It has lost whatever it used to have – the spark – if it ever had it. The dilemma and the compromise are more profound. I saw that art and the repression, for instance, when I was working at the Institut del Teatre in Barcelona with Joan J. Guillèn. And of course, one can think of other places of oppression and tyranny – like the art made during the Second World War in the Nazi concentration camp of Terezín (Theresienstadt): drawing, making music and performing for one's life, whether it was Shakespeare, Calderón, Hans Krása's children's opera *Brundibár* or Verdi's *Requiem*. What is that if not subversion, a symbol of defiance? I believe that's what artists have to do.

One of the most memorable moments from *The Ballad of the Cosmo Café* is that although it takes place in a café – where people meet and keep company, in a café that is a hub of social life – the people there are all lonely: the ghost of Sigmund Freud, the three ladies all living in their past dreams, Pammy coming in on her own, meeting the painter Lewandowsky – another lonely figure. *The Unicorn and Joe* is also about a lonely boy. And so is *Charlotte* about a lonely artist. In Pavel Haas's opera *Šarlatán* – one of my as yet-unrealised dreams – the once famous quack doctor Pustrpalk ends up entirely on his own, misunderstood. They were all lonely people. The loneliness is in many ways the reverse side of freedom, especially for the artist. To be an artist of any sort is a really tough job because one has to find a way of not knowing what one is doing – which I think is hugely important – but also being at ease with oneself and being able to communicate with oneself. As an artist, unlike other employments, one can't depend on the validation from others. For this, one needs an absolute self-discipline: I come to work at ten in the morning, I finish at a certain time and I am very strict about it – but I've had to learn that. I also had to learn to accept isolation and loneliness. Some people don't believe it: they think artists are having a party all the time.

This is what we say – from the Hebrew Ethics of the Fathers:

If I am not for myself, who will be?
If I am only for myself, what am I?
And if not now, when?

When I was teaching a class at the University of California in Los Angeles, I wrote this poem. It is about the loneliness, isolation and misunderstanding one encounters everywhere:

LEAVING

I'm leaving the land
Where no one understands me
And returning to the land
Where I am misunderstood

No more Paradise Cove
Where the clams and mussells are poisoned
Farewell my lovely
Wilshire Boulevard
Building, where from
The High Window of my apartment I can see
The final Temple, stained glass and white tower
Its base the Holy Ark
Its spire reaching into the dark
Of the Big Sleep

The Long Goodbye to Nieman-Marcus
1 dollar 35 cents on the 21 bus
where The Simple Art of Murder is
the easiest way to grab a sales bargain
From anorexic women dressed like
The Lady in the Lake
Dragged up from Pacific Palisades,
with hair a straight playback to the 1960s
and usually accompanied by a very plain
Little Sister.
And so, I leave the land
Where no one understands me,
To return to the land
Where Trouble seems to be my Business
And I am constantly misunderstood.

THE PAPER
DRESS
ARRIVES

I have always surrounded myself with significant objects that have a history and a poetry. During the war years of rationing, the arrival of boxes from Jackie – containing Hershey's chocolate bars, children's books, clothes, dried foods and often something special for me – were beyond excitement. There was no internet or phones, so post was eagerly awaited. Cousin Jackie was the daughter of my grandmother's older sister. With another sister they had been unceremoniously disembarked in Newcastle upon Tyne in England. They searched for the Statue of Liberty, and they realised they had been cheated. Eventually, after several weeks of dossing down in dockers' dormitories, they managed to get a passage to America. They lived in Brooklyn in New York, where they became American citizens and dyed their hair blue. Later they moved to Columbus, Ohio and Florida. I first met these aunts in 1958 when I got married and they came to the wedding.

Many years later, in 2006, in another life – out of the blue – I had a phone call from the dean of Theatre at Carnegie Mellon University in Pittsburgh. She had read the first edition of *What is Scenography?* and told me that the department was applying for funds for an artist in residence and wondered if I had a project that I would like to develop. I had no hesitation in offering from my Arsenal of Dreams the short one-act comic opera by the Czech composer Bohuslav Martinů. I had directed and created the scenography for Martinů's great tragic opera *The Greek Passion* a few years before in Thessaloniki in the Heptapyrgion Fortress – the town's former prison, now a UNESCO World Heritage site. With the help of the wonderful Martinů Institute in Prague, while teaching at DAMU (the Theatre Academy of Performing Arts), I had been able to spend time researching other operas he had composed while living in exile in New York. I discovered that in 1953, Serge Koussevitzky, the music director of the Boston Symphony Orchestra, had helped Martinů obtain a commission to write a chamber opera for the NBC television series *Opera for All*. The television series was created by Sam Chotzinoff – himself an émigré. Martinů took *The Wedding* – also known as *The Marriage* – a two-act play written by Nikolai Gogol, another exile and wanderer, and composed music for a one-hour comic opera *The Marriage* (*Ženitba*).

Gogol's story is set in the early nineteenth century, and as devotee of Gogol's writing I proposed to CMU a research project to investigate how a television opera might be staged. The proposal was

accepted, and in the Autumn of 2006 I went to CMU in Pittsburgh to work with students on the MFA in Theatre Design course aiming to stage three fragments under the title *Martinů in America*. I was offered a space on the second floor of the Regina Gouger Miller Gallery. On the first and third floors, an exhibition of installation artists was in preparation. I went to survey the space with some of the students, and we thought we could take advantage of the gallery space and bring a performative element into the installation, provided we could install a small piano and a pianist. The excellent music department at CMU were happy to help us with both.

One day while walking to the university, I found in the street outside a grand Scottish-style house an old American refrigerator. I looked at it for some time, and then asked someone from the theatre workshop to go and pick it up for me. My aunts had told us that when émigrés obtained American citizenship, they were presented with a refrigerator, a washing machine, a Hoover, a large carton of Tide washing powder and an American flag. This now-redundant object spoke to me – it brought back a memory. When my grandmother died in 1964, I went with my parents back to the little house in Acanthus Avenue in Newcastle upon Tyne to clear the house. There was the small refrigerator that my mother had persuaded her to buy. When we opened it, it contained – her china! I stored this image in the arsenal of my mind, along with all those memories of my early childhood.

And then, decades later, in the streets of Pittsburgh, it came to me that Gogol's story, which became Martinů's comic opera *The Marriage,* could easily be updated to New York in 1957 and become a familiar story of how people can adapt from one life to the next. With the students, we set out collecting old objects that 'told a story' and eventually, when the gallery became available, installing them in the space. I found some old dishwasher-proof china made in America, put it inside the refrigerator and left its door slightly ajar.

On the last day before the opening of our performance piece, visitors to the other two installations were invited to come in to ours and look around. Suddenly I heard a voice shouting: *Who has done THIS?* I looked up and saw a man who was gazing into the refrigerator. *I have done this,* I replied. *My grandmother kept her china in her refrigerator. – NO!* he shouted across the gallery, *MY grandmother used to do that and I have NEVER told anyone!* – and he walked out.

After the exploratory production at Carnegie Mellon University, the china came back to England with me and is in my kitchen now, a daily memory of this event and our production.

When I was in Pittsburgh, I met Jay Bolotin, a multidisciplinary artist, who became one of the greatest inspirations to me. Bolotin is a

Russian Jewish name, and Jay's grandfather was a religious thinker, a rabbi, who settled in Kentucky and ironically became the biggest pig farmer in the region. Jay grew up on this pig farm. As an artist, Jay makes woodcuts, films and puppets, writes plays and songs, is a musician, draws, paints – and is a man of all trades. His art has great relevance to my work – he also has dreams, and he carries them out. Another thing we have in common is *la quotidienne* – our love for objects of the everyday. Like me, he elevates the everyday into art. I don't necessarily make big, grand works but I could take an ordinary object and make art with it – if an object has history and a story. Elevating that object into art not because it's fancy work but because it's part of the mixture, an ingredient of making theatre or visual artwork – like if you are cooking. Jay does the same, and he sometimes says that we artists are all cooks and we make a feast for others to enjoy.

In 2009, I was invited by the Janáček Opera at the National Theatre in Brno in the Czech Republic to offer something as part of the Martinů Revisited Festival. The artistic director of the opera took me to see the historic Reduta Theatre in the Market Place Square (Zelný trh), and told me this was the place where Mozart had performed and that, allegedly, he first tried out his opera *The Magic Flute* in the theatre – and sure enough there is a statue of Mozart flying in the air in front of this beautiful classic building from the early 1730s. On the first floor are grand floor-to-ceiling windows (called Piano Nobile) in a room used as a concert recital hall. There is also a modern auditorium at the back of the hall. It was there that the organizers proposed to stage *The Marriage*. As we were walking through all the rooms, I had a vision of this story – but not told in a theatre but in a space that would exactly contrast with the opera's characters. I politely asked if it would be possible to stage *The Marriage* in the Mozart concert hall, and the chief technician who was accompanying the opera director and myself said emphatically: *No! This is a heritage floor that Mozart walked on!* I promised not to do anything that could harm the floor, and to put floor coverings under all the installed pieces. I made a very quick drawing the next day, as I imagined it, and then dared to ask the most important question: *Could the audience sit the length of the salon facing the Piano Nobile windows, instead of as normal, facing the end by the piano?* And moreover: *Could the seats be made of a collection of odd chairs?* This was an image

I treasured and knew from the photos of immigrants waiting in the admissions room at Ellis Island. I had collected copies of the photos from the Museum of the Holocaust in Washington DC. In this excellent museum, I learned that from 1949 to 1955 the huge influx of immigrants to America had subsided. Ellis Island, while still functioning as a processing centre, had fallen into disrepair, and the US Coast Guard were using it for office and storage space. In the 1950s, there was a sudden resurgence of immigrants landing at Ellis Island, and urgent renovations and repairs had to be made. The office published appeals to the public to donate old chairs for the reception room, and many were obtained. This eclectic mixture of chairs gave me the idea, and I wished to reproduce this image as the audience seating, so that the characters in the opera were looking at the chairs of Ellis Island that they saw as the first thing the moment they arrived in America. My production of *The Marriage* has had several different revivals but always told the same story of displacement and home away from home.

I am often asked how I was able to capture the characters in the story so accurately. The truth is that they are all memories of my family from my childhood days in Newcastle upon Tyne – a memory never forgotten. It is as though I unpacked a cardboard box of memories sent during those dark days from Cousin Jackie to brighten our lives.

I visited Prague over many years, often teaching scenography to students at DAMU. Prague is a city of music, and opposite to the entrance to DAMU was a music shop, with music blaring out into the narrow Karlova Street. One day I went into the shop and asked what that music was that they were just then playing. And that was how I discovered Martinů – hearing the string quartets. I remembered a saying of Marc Chagall that I had on my bedroom wall: *When colour is right – form is right . . . colour is vibration . . . like music.* Martinů's music has always attracted me because it is so unlike the romantic-nationalistic melodies of Dvořák and Smetana. He seemed to be living in the twentieth century with a truly individual sound. Then I found a small book about Martinů that included pages of his drawings in pencil and colour, not as conventional artworks, but as thinking drawings expressing both the joy and frustration of creation. At that point, I did not know that 'fate' was going to bring me into his world. But a dream appeared.

I was a frequent visitor to the University of Visual Arts during the years of reconstruction in Belgrade in Serbia, and I suggested making a performance piece based on the 1918 event at the Cabaret Voltaire, where the Dadaists led by Tristan Tzara held an event demonstrating all the clashing art forms. This was a metaphor for the turbulent and chaotic time of the First World War. I was offered an empty space in the Dorćol, the former Jewish district leading to the lower banks of the Danube. The building used to be a synagogue, then the Rex Cinema and, finally, a disused space. Here we created the first *SCENOMANIFESTO!* to music, with groups representing all the elements of making theatre that finally all came together in a dance with the audience. We gave three performances. Unknown to me, the great costume designer Ioanna Manoledaki from Thessaloniki was at the Belgrade Opera, and she came to see our *SCENOMANIFESTO!* Afterwards she introduced herself and explained she was also the chair of the Board of Directors of the National Opera of Northern Greece, and asked me if I would like to propose a production for them. She suggested *La Traviata* or *La Bohème* – neither of which I wanted to do. But I had a dream from my days in Prague where I had heard the wonderful music – albeit on headphones in a cubicle in the record shop – of Martinů's great opera *The Greek Passion*, based on Nikos Kazantzakis's book *Christ Recrucified*. I supposed this to be a staple of Greek opera repertoire, and to my astonishment I discovered that it had never been translated into Greek, as Kazantzakis had been exiled from Greece for committing the offence of blasphemy against the church. I hoped my opportunity had come, and tentatively proposed this to the opera house. Amazingly, the suggestion was accepted, and Ioanna herself decided to make the translation.

I was invited to visit Thessaloniki, to see the opera house and meet the technical team, and here the trouble began. The theatre was a wide narrow envelope proscenium. The commonly performed second version of *The Greek Passion* starts and ends in a church, but the first version, which I wanted to stage, is all set in the open air in the courtyard of the church and on the mountain of Sarakina. I could not bear the idea of making a false open-air courtyard, and I asked if it was possible to find an alternative space. Luckily the production manager had a car, and he offered to drive me round Thessaloniki to show me several spaces – all of which he assured me would be unsuitable for a production requiring a large orchestra. Then my young assistant and interpreter suggested we go up the steep hill dominating the city and have a look at the eleventh-century Byzantine citadel, which was formerly the town's prison. The citadel was built from two opposing towers enclosing a courtyard space with a small entrance to the inner part of the building. Steep steps on the outside of the left-hand tower led to a gallery overlooking the whole site. The space was perfect for the story. *The Greek Passion* tells of the conflict between the Greeks and the Turks, who have become the rulers of the fictional village of Lycrovissi. I could see how the two towers of the citadel could represent the two communities, who had somehow learned to co-exist. We climbed to the top where I imagined the Turkish Governor could survey the scene and looked over the sea and Mount Olympus in the distance – and one could almost see Zeus and Hera in the clouds in the sky arguing and fighting with each other as Greek myths tell. I was totally excited and inspired and was sure that this was the space we needed. The problem was how to convince the Guardians of the site.

I knew the writings of Kazantzakis, albeit in translation, and loved his larger-than-life representation of humanity. I read *Christ Recrucified* and discovered a book full of moral indignation combined with, as Kazantzakis says, *Good spirits, humour, ordinary 'human' everyday talk, laughter, jokes with plenty of salt, difficult concepts formulated with peasant simplicity.* (See also the second edition of *What is Scenography?*, p. 144.) Its universality asks readers to consider what has sadly become the burning question all over the world: What would you do if a fellow citizen, a stranger, asks for your help? Do you act, or do you say, *Not in my backyard*, as most of us might well do? Martinů and Kazantzakis were exiles in France, when they created this music drama. I felt it spoke so personally to me that I had vowed that one day I would create a production where life and art would meet.

I hoped that my experience as a visual artist in the theatre could bring Kazantzakis's characters to life on the stage. It seemed to me that I really knew these people – the villagers of the imagined Lycovrissi. I knew from my own heritage – the world of the refugees – of people living their lives until they suddenly find themselves 'ethnically cleansed', driven out and forced to wander, carrying what possessions they can. Exile affects all, old and young, women and men, the sick and the feeble. We see it every day in the papers and on television, but it is always someone else's problem until it arrives on our doorstep. The parable Kazantzakis uses to tell this story is the Easter Passion. He shows the profound changes that occur as the chosen actors in the Passion Play gradually become the characters they are supposed to be representing. When Manolios, who plays Christ, is finally killed, he becomes a hero, but the question arises: Is heroism any use to the homeless? The question remains, and it is left to Pope Fotis (the Bringer of Light) to lead his wretched flock including starving children to a new life in yet another place. After my first trip to the citadel in Thessaloniki, I had to return to England the next day, my head buzzing with the dreams and ideas about how we could obtain permission to use this space.

Back in England, a few days later, I was walking down one of the main streets in Chichester, when I passed a well-known music and record shop that was closing down. Outside was a large open black garbage bin, and I noticed that it was full of empty CD cases. Luckily I had a large empty shopping bag, and to the shop owner's amusement I filled it with the CD cases. At that moment, I only thought that they might come in useful. When I emptied the bag onto my drawing table in the studio, they seemed to be looking at me saying: *Cut some card, make an image and send them to Thessaloniki.* My grandchildren had been visiting me. I had some children's modelling clay in red, yellow and blue plasticene, and I had been showing them how many different colours one can make by rubbing different colours together – a skill I had learned during the war on plasticene from Cousin Jackie. We had some amusement making little animals, and then they went home leaving everything for me to clear up. Idly I cut some thin card to the size of the CD case and with a palette knife spread the green-black clay over the card. This awakened a memory of all the different tones of black I had noticed when visiting the villages outside Thessaloniki. Black, faded in the sun, or from too much washing – a different black according to silk, linen, cotton. The words *a Symphony of Blacks* came into my head.

In my extensive storage in the studio, I found the box marked 'Balkan Drawings' – for I never go out without a sketchbook and a pencil in my bag – and there again were children's eyes looking at me. I noticed that people's eyes were all individual. And I still do start a face with two eyes. Many years later, while travelling through and teaching in Balkan countries, I drew groups of Roma children in Bucharest, in Northern Greece and again in Spain in Triana on the other side of the river to Barcelona city. There I learned that *eyes are the windows of the soul. The Greek Passion* has a large chorus of children, so my collection of drawings of children was a gift from my arsenal. With a surgical scalpel I began to scrape away the plasticene on the card, and it was almost like the characters of *The Greek Passion* had been incarcerated under the plasticene on the card and were being released.

For the next few days, I worked feverishly scraping and cutting, listening to Martinů's score, until I had nearly all the characters. It was thrilling. I packed them up in their CD cases, went to the post office and sent them express to Ioanna Manoledaki at the National Opera of Northern Greece. A week later, she phoned me in great excitement proposing to send me an air ticket to come immediately to Thessaloniki, and we would go together back to the Eptapyrigion to obtain permission to stage our opera there. I asked her not to show them to anyone until I arrived, for I felt in some strange mythological way the Greek goddesses of Fate – the Moirai – might be watching over me.

The appointed day came, and we went up the single path in a taxi (the only way to get there) and entered the governor's room. He was sitting behind a great mahogany table surrounded by several other men, all of whom looked as if they could be characters in the opera. After the usual formal greetings and saying nothing, I spread out the drawings on the table, and through Sakis, our interpreter, I said: *This is what I intend to do here.* We sat down, and the governor and his gentlemen picked them up and passed them around. After merely fifteen minutes of total silence, they all nodded, and he said simply: *Yes. You may come, but you must not touch the historic Byzantine wall.* We thanked him and without further conversation departed. We then looked at this wall that defined the courtyard area, and realised we would have to build a seating block for 600 spectators around it without touching it, and here I heard those magic Greek words: *No problem! We'll do it!!* Those drawings in the CD cases had more power than any verbal argument could ever have done. They are frequently requested for exhibitions and are displayed against a wall close together, referencing Greco-Roman mosaics in the Rotunda in the city of Thessaloniki.

Presenting *The Greek Passion* in this historic monument of a medieval fortress-turned-prison, whose stones tell stories and hold

"EYES ARE THE WINDOWS of the SOUL"

DRAWING OF ROMA CHILDREN IN
THESSALONIKI.. .. ...

strong resonances that awaken our collective memory, was the start of my future journey. Here the universality of the Kazantzakis-Martinů creation seemed to have found a perfect home. The space speaks, and difficult concepts can be expressed with the direct simplicity embodied in the text, the music and the wonderful use of light, created by the great and much-missed late theatre and architectural lighting designer Henk van der Geest, who so tragically died in 2019, well before his time. My theatre work has evolved from a theatre designer to a *sculptor of the stage space*. I find less and less need for scenery. I am more concerned with making the most of architectural spaces, creating simple, strong stagings that really tell the story.

When we were working in Toronto on *Charlotte: A Tri-Coloured Play with Music* with Alon Nashman and Aleš Březina, I needed to find a suitable period summer dress for the singer playing Charlotte, and with enough movement in it to be able to fit other singers of similar stature who might come into the cast. I searched many vintage shops and could not find anything appropriate. Then I remembered what I had in a store somewhere in the loft of my house – something I had carefully wrapped in the paper that came in the American box all those years ago from my mother's cousin Jackie in Brooklyn: A PAPER DRESS! I found it and happily it fitted all our changing Charlottes perfectly. I donated a vintage straw hat I never wore to complete the image of this young girl painting for her life as she sensed that time was running out for her.

The last and final outing of our much-lauded production was at the Nová scéna of the National Opera in Prague in June 2019. I was glad to be back in Prague, which I consider my adopted second home. I walked from my apartment to the Malostranská metro and tram station, and to my total amazement I confronted a huge poster advertising our production on the wall – and there was the singer Adanya Dunn wearing my mother's paper dress (and my straw hat). Furthermore, when I took the tram to the Opera House, inside the tram was a smaller version. I looked at it for the entire journey, and thought about that moment during my early wartime childhood when that big box arrived on the doorstep of 74 Acanthus Avenue, Newcastle upon Tyne, and my mother found the paper dress and my grandmother stoutly declared: *You can't wear that!!* – and although my mother never did, the dress itself defied history, and fate brought it to life – in our production of *Charlotte: A Tri-Coloured Play with Music* as it was performed across the world.

Being an artist is not a one-off project but a way of life. It is a lifelong project. I never really thought about making a living as an objective in my life, partly because I was a 'child bride' (as I call myself): my parents' anxiety that I wouldn't get married because I was too independent and therefore I wouldn't be able to make a living – because people believed that a girl had to be married to someone in order to thrive! That was a fact of life for many people of my generation. I can't say about other people or make claims about how one lives now. I was never wealthy, and it's never been my motivation in life. Some young artists find the pressures too great and decide to find a more stable job – but some of them also end up finding their way back to the arts later.

If one has a dream where they want to be in ten years' time, they can't be there now, but they can work towards it. Edward Gordon Craig never could realise what he wanted until he was ninety. One has to think of it as a long journey and be prepared to go on that journey: one never finishes where one started off. And especially an artist's life is full of unexpected surprises and adventures.

Surprises come with art – the journey is never straightforward as it takes metaphoric leaps – for metaphors make connections that are profound and often surprising and far from obvious. The metaphor goes beyond mere reality to some hidden secret. And that is certainly true of scenography. Ralph Koltai was a great advocate of the visual metaphor, and he never wanted to reproduce reality on stage. He always claimed that one could always do it much better in real life. When he worked with the filmmaker Ken Russell (1927–2011), Ken would say to Ralph very adamantly: *Now look here, Ralph.* And Ralph told me that whenever he heard Ken utter those words, he knew that there would be trouble. Once, when they were working on Bernd Alois Zimmermann's 1960 opera *Die Soldaten*, Ken also said those ominous words and added: *On that stage, I just want three platforms. Just give me one in the middle and one either side.* When Ralph was telling me about it, he said, *When I heard that, my heart sank. But then I thought: I'll show him.* He made a maquette of a naked woman's torso and cut it into three so that on the first platform the actors came through her breast, on the second through her legs, and on the third through part of her head, just above the lips. Nonetheless, they were proper platforms with steps at the back for actors to enter. The genius of the design is that Ralph's visual metaphor synchronized with the world of Zimmermann's opera. In the end, the scenography told more than the score or the opera's libretto. In the totality of the work, these weren't three separate platforms but a beautiful unified image – and when the audience saw a woman's naked torso cut into three, they somehow knew the world that it came from. The metaphor is powerful and reveals a lot of meaning, and took the art on another, unexpected adventure.

This example says even more: it encapsulates one of the biggest questions of art – its usefulness. Art takes us beyond the obvious and brings to us something unexpected. It surprises us, takes us on an adventure and tells us something new. That is in my view truly useful, and I often ask my students to do the same: *Show me something that I didn't know I wanted to see.*

Sometime around 1990, I was walking across the Charles Bridge in Prague with my friend and colleague, the artist, painter, boat lover and scenographer Jaroslav Malina (1937–2016). The dark clouds of Europe were lifting, and we were both teaching at DAMU (Theatre Academy of Performing Arts). I had not seen my old friend for some years, and it was a joyful reunion. We stopped at the centre of the bridge and looked at River Vltava flowing fast – Smetana's *Má vlast* dedicated to the river is as well known as the sound of freedom – and I said to him, quoting Annie Lennox's song: *Sweet dreams are made of this!* He replied thoughtfully: *Do you think that we could create a scenography master's course for mature students to come together from any country, and make work together?* Without hesitation, I replied, *Why not? Prague is the centre of the scenographic world and we all come here for the Prague Quadrennial every four years.*

In 1987, I had become course director of Theatre Design at Central Saint Martins College of Art and Design, at that time part of the London Institute. The department had a tradition of unconventional and experimental artistic practice, and had commissioned the Jeanetta Cochrane Theatre to be built as part of our historic building in Central London. I wanted to be adventurous and forward-looking and thought this could be one original pathway. I spoke to the vice dean for International Affairs at DAMU, Barbara Tůmová, and she was so enthusiastic. I vowed that on my return to London I would speak to the principal of Central and see what support there might be. The time was right economically to develop master's courses, and I wrote to all the theatre design courses I knew giving a date and asked who would come to a lunch and a meeting to discuss this 'at their own cost'. Forty people responded. From that, I contacted four heads of courses I knew – and as I had hoped, a development group was formed: Iago Pericot (Institut del Teatre, Barcelona), Henny Dörr (HKU University of the Arts Utrecht), Barbara Tůmová (DAMU, Prague), Maija Pekkanen (Alvo Aalto Arts University, Helsinki) and myself for Central Saint Martins College of Art and Design in London. We conceived a simple plan of an intensive one-year course to be delivered over forty-eight weeks. Admission to the course, which could come from any discipline, was based on writing a 'dream proposal': *If I could take a year out of my life I would . . .* and then the applicants were to add their dream. Its purpose was to give artists space, resources and support to develop their dream into a possible actuality through systematic research, meeting people from other cultures and creating through staged workshops a 'passport' or 'Modell-Buch'. They could then offer them for a full realization to companies in the outside world.

On the course, the students could elect to start in one centre for three months, move to another centre for three months and return to their home centre for the final three. The international faculty would also rotate. Each centre offered a different specialization: Prague focused on music, Helsinki on film, Barcelona on street theatre, Utrecht on contemporary dance – and later Zürich joined with their specialization in architecture. And thus the European Scenography Centres (ESC) were born, though it took four years to incubate. Thinking of Ariane Mnouchkine's words that *Theatre should be a celebration*, I planned that each year would begin and end with a festival in a different centre at which students in one year could pass the baton on to their new colleagues and of course to the public. Thus, SCENOFEST! entered the scenographic vocabulary. One of the objectives we had written in the funding for our 'dream' that became the ESC was to create an international community of scenographers who would know each other, support each other and make work together. And although the ESC project no longer exists, our former students, many now in major positions in theatre and academic institutions, still carry this ethic on.

As part of the European Scenography Centres programme, we set up a tradition: once a month a student would receive some money and cook lunch from their national cuisine. For that lunch, I would always invite someone from the profession to come and sit at the table with the students – which goes back to my own cultural tradition that we always leave a place at the table for a guest. And of course, if any of the students had parents visiting at that point, they could bring them in. Until it was discontinued by health and safety regulations, this brilliant ritual contributed greatly to the learning and to the community. It created a home from home for the students, because sometimes it was quite hard on the individuals who may have felt uprooted or homesick. In Prague, we had an arrangement with a café around the corner from the Theatre Academy (DAMU), and we would contribute to the costs of the events that students hosted there.

We used English as our common means of communication, but we also did more to create a shared language. On arriving in their

first centre, their 'home base', the students were asked to bring three books with them – in their own language, with illustrations – and put them into our small reference library: a bookshelf in our office. They could then take the books back home when they completed the degree, but most of them left them for others. That idea allowed students to use the photographs and the reproductions in the book as windows into their own cultures and as points of reference to make themselves understood as creators.

There were many memorable moments in the European Scenography Centres. One moment I keep coming back to involves two students who met there and became collaborators. One was from Korea and her primary interest was in visual choreography. Her home base centre was Utrecht – at the time very prominent in contemporary dance. The other student was from Japan, with an interest in photography and lighting. Several years later, I went to Korea and saw a dance piece they had created together and was deeply moved by it – thinking of the long history of animosity between their two countries. And here, two young people are making work together and couldn't have done this if we hadn't opened the door for them in the European Scenography Centres. At that point, I thought that all the dragging off to Brussels to negotiate the transfer of credits, all the paperwork needed for the validation and all the toil that had to go into realizing this impossible dream – all of it was worth it. These two people made work together. I have also been in touch with many other former students from the programme. Many have become world-leading artists in their respective fields – from scenography, through video art or photography, to museology. I feel truly honoured to have helped give opportunities to them. Many of them became my close friends – among them Edwin Erminy, with whom we set up Opera Transatlántica. The ESC was also an invaluable opportunity to work with wonderful people and get to know their cultures – from Prague and Utrecht to the Catalan culture in Barcelona. It was a team effort, and the success of the programme is testimony to all the wonderful people who made the dream come true.

In 1994, I was once again teaching at DAMU. I love being in Prague because it is so easy to walk everywhere. At this time, many buildings that had fallen into disrepair were being renovated, and the city was waking up again. I went to the National Museum with the intention of seeing their theatre collection. What I saw

astonished me and in one way changed my life. At the entrance
to the gallery stood an open, old battered suitcase. Standing in
the suitcase was a mannequin, dressed in an old bed sheet, with
pieces of torn lace petticoats attached to it. A large necklace
made of flattened food tins strung together with bits of wire and
a crown similarly made completed the figure of King Ahasuerus
for the folk play of *Esther*. In the gallery were more drawings by
František Zelenka (1904–44), dated 1943 and 1944. I knew of
Zelenka's work as an architect, interior designer, graphic posters
and filmmaker – a typical polymath artist of the 1920s and 1930s.
A lady came to stand by me and, noticing my shock, introduced
herself as Vlasta Koubská, curator of the exhibition and head of the
National Museum's Theatre Collection Department. She told me
that when the ghetto of Terezín (the Nazi concentration camp north
of Prague) was being reconstructed for new housing development,
the builders digging up a road had found the suitcases buried in the
ground with the costume and all the drawings that were from the
time when Jews were incarcerated in the Terezín camp before being
transported to their deaths in Auschwitz in 1944. I asked Vlasta if
she thought it would be possible to bring the exhibition to London,
and I explained to her that this could be the first SCENOFEST! to
open the European Scenography Centres. *If you can find the money*,
she smiled, *then we will do it*. The next day I took a bus to Terezín
with Barbara Tůmová, and we walked around and looked at the
road where the suitcases were unearthed, and she offered to become
the liaison with the Museum and the Lethaby Gallery in Central
London that was part of our Art College.

When I got back to London feverish with excitement, I contacted
Sylvia Backmeyer, chief librarian and curator of the gallery. She
immediately suggested going back to Prague so she could see the
exhibition and meet her counterpart Vlasta Koubská. A meeting was
arranged a few days later at Barbara's apartment in Národní Street
in Prague. Back in London, I co-opted the services of a well-known
actress with a good phone voice to start a fundraising initiative. She
took over my office and within three weeks raised £56,000! There
was no going back. This would indeed be a spectacular opening for
the first cohort of ESC. The exhibition ran during 5–23 September
1994. I separated the two rooms of the Lethaby Gallery by fixing
a torn black gauze curtain across the entire width of the space. As
visitors entered, they saw the early works of Zelenka loaned from

the archives of the National Museum Prague, National Theatre Prague, the Museum of Applied Arts Prague, the State Jewish Museum Prague and the Terezín National Monument. The suitcase with King Ahasuerus rising up from it was in the centre. Visitors then had to walk through the torn black gauze curtain to view the works produced in the Theatre in the Attic in the Terezín ghetto. Music played.

Large posters were displayed on the boards down Southampton Row. On the day before the opening, an elderly lady hesitantly came into the gallery. She explained that she was just passing and hoped she would be allowed to see it. She had a Czech accent in English. We welcomed her, explaining we were just putting the finishing touches to the exhibition. She walked around and went through the black gauze curtain. Suddenly we heard a scream; fearing she had an accident, we ran to see. She was clutching the wall and crying in front of Zelenka's costume design of *Esther*: *That was me*, she said. *I was a young actress at the National Theatre before I was taken . . . I survived.*

The next day we welcomed the first cohort of twelve international MA students on the European Scenography Centres course starting at the London centre. Then two well-dressed gentlemen arrived and asked to speak to me. They were (in a private capacity) the playwright Václav Havel (1936–2011), then president of the Czech Republic and the Czech minister of culture and writer Pavel Tigrid (1917–2003). They gave me a small box containing a ring of Czech garnets, a bracelet of garnets and a gold Star of David with garnets that I have never taken off since that day. The BBC 3 Music broadcaster Christopher Cook was head of Cultural Studies at Central Saint Martins College of Art and Design, and he came and listened to the stories that were in the air. We immediately decided to have some evening talks; one them was dedicated to 'The Music of Terezín' – and that was the introduction of 'forbidden music' to the British public.

Pavel Tigrid had written the foreword to the catalogue we produced for this exhibition, which concludes with these words:

The exhibition at the Lethaby Gallery is also the contribution of Czech stage design to the international stage design forum SCENOFEST!, organised on the occasion of the opening of the first year of the Master of Arts Course in Scenography. To my great delight it also marks the collaboration between Central Saint Martins College of Art and Design and the European Scenography Centres with the Academy of Music and Dramatic Arts in Prague.

A dream was realised, and out of the ashes, like Ravel's Angel, came Zelenka's symbol of hope.

One day I was working at DAMU in Prague and I just had to get out of the building and went for a walk along the River Vltava. I came to Jan Palach Square and the impressive neo-classicist concert hall, the Rudolfinum. I saw that a concert was shortly to begin. I went in and bought a ticket, simply thinking I could sit quietly and regain my strength. I bought a programme, and I saw it was a conductor from Berlin, Israel Yinon (1956–2015), and the programme was the music of composers, many of whom had been sent from Terezín to the extermination camp in Auschwitz in October 1944. We heard music by Viktor Ullmann (1898–1944) and Erwin Schulhoff (1894–1942), and the piece that moved me most was the *Šarlátan* Suite by Pavel Haas (1899–1944), whose memorial I had visited in Brno. I was totally transfixed and wished to meet this wild-haired, intense and spirited man who was conducting the concert and find out more. At the end of the concert, there was tumultuous applause from the audience, and with a head reeling with the sounds I exited by a side door. As I was going down the staircase, I bumped into Maestro Yinon, dared to introduce myself and tell him how moved I was by the concert. We sat by the river in the cool evening light and spoke. I admitted that I loved especially the *Šarlatán* Suite by Pavel Haas. He told me that originally *Šarlatán* had been written for the main opera house in Brno, the Mahen Theatre, built in the Viennese style, which was the first major opera house to have electricity! And then he said to me seriously: *My dream is to stage* Šarlatán *as a chamber opera in a flexible space that visually reflects the ravages in Europe of the Thirty Years' War*. That idea really interested me. We parted vowing to keep in touch.

In 2012, I was invited to propose a performance project at the Royal Scottish Conservatoire in Glasgow, and without any hesitation I suggested rewriting and staging parts of Haas's *Šarlatán* as a chamber opera working with Pavel Drábek as librettist and Israel Yinon as maestro, with the conservatoire music and theatre

FRANTIŠEK ZELENKA
1904-1944

"ASH"
L'ENFANT et les SORTILÈGES
— MAURICE RAVEL —
PRAGUE NATIONAL THEATRE
1927

Frantisek Zelenka. An artist of Jewish origins, he was eventually forbidden to work
and taken to the Terrezin ghetto. However, not even there did he succumb
to the tragic fate and, together with other artists, he awoke in the camp faith in life
and its further fulfilment. Frantisek Zelenka died in the autumn of 1944
along with tens of thousands of other Jewish prisoners.

Pavel Tigrid
Minister for Culture of the Czech Republic

1994

students. Yinon told the students that *Music is about emotion, about feeling, about the time where we are now, and the time of the past, about society and working together.* We also had the services of the Scottish poet Alexander Hutchison (1943–2015), who was a Royal Literary Fellow, and he told us all about the Scottish mercenaries who were employed by the Swedes to ravage the fields of people in Europe, as Brecht describes in his seminal play *Mother Courage*. And so it came to pass, we performed a few scenes from the opera, and every moment was thrilling. We presented our final results to invited audiences and hoped that a company somewhere would take it up and fully develop it. That did not happen, but we all vowed to dream and store it away in our arsenals of future projects.

On 29 January 2015, I was in Ljubljana beginning my early work on *Carmen*, when I received a phone call with terrible news. Maestro Israel Yinon had died while conducting an orchestral concert at the Luzern Festival. He was midway through Richard Strauss's *Alpine Symphony*, and when the music reaches its full climax, he collapsed and fell dead into the orchestra pit. His girlfriend was playing the oboe in the orchestra. A short time later, we got news that Sandy Hutchison had died unexpectedly, and we decided to temporarily shelve the *Šarlatán* project but to keep it in our Arsenal of Dreams until the time would be right. I wrote this poem to console myself on hearing the terrible news of our friend's passing:

DEATH OF YINON

Too Late
It's always too late
Meant to phone
Meant to write
Thought about it
In the night
It's always too late

Golden haired
In Switzerland he fell
Trumpets sounding
From his rock he plunged
Into the pit below
And it was too late

Proud, generous and fierce
Israel fought
For those who could not sing
His baton a sword
The podium
His stage, and people heard.

And now those thoughts
Put off for a day
Are just words on a list
Smudged with tears
Too late, too late, too late.
It always is too late.

Thursday January 29th 2015, Ljubjana
On the tragic death of Maestro Israel Yinon aged 59

This poem is written in imitation of a famous poem for Joseph Trumpeldor (1880–1920), one of the early pioneers to Palestine, who was standing on a rock called Jaffa that became Tel Aviv. Legend has it that when they found his body, trumpets sounded. My poem follows the rhythm of the song. Maestro Israel Yinon had an artistic voice, and he used it. We shared a lot – from our constant resistance to tyranny to loneliness. He once told me: *I was an outsider in Israel and I am an outsider in Berlin*. We also shared the sentiment that has accompanied me all my life: *I come from somewhere but I belong nowhere*.

All things come to pass, and the one dream that is consistent in my arsenal of projects is to find ways of using my visual art to *let the eyes see what the ears do not hear* – one of the dictums of the actor/director/visual artist and pioneering theorist Edward Gordon Craig in his book *On the Art of Theatre* (1911). For dreams to come true, one needs to find the time and work for them. Especially now that eternity is not on my side – as I often say.

I regulate my time. I start work at ten in the morning, and I stop at six at night. I've come to realise that knowing when to stop is very important and very hard. It has taken me a lifetime to understand that. Sometimes my instinct drives me to go on and on. I could work till midnight, get very tired and make a mess of it. But another little voice in my head says: *Stop it. Go to the sea.* I then usually walk down to the shore, look at the tide and think: *The tide comes in, and the tide comes out, and tomorrow is another day.* I am lucky to live by the sea because the tide helps me to keep the time. Coming here to this house near the sea has helped me understand time much more. It also helped me learn to manage my time in ways I couldn't when I was younger and living elsewhere.

I time myself by BBC Radio 3 programmes nowadays. I say to myself that I need to finish a task by the afternoon concert, for instance. This gives rhythm to my day. The more I listen to music, the more I learn about time – something we have often discussed with the composer Aleš Březina – because if I listen to a symphony, say, Mahler's Third Symphony, that listening happens *in time*, and my drawing synchronizes with the music and comes to move hand in hand with it.

I have to have organization in my life. I need to have all my domestic things ready at night so that I can wake up in the morning with nothing left over from the day before except the work that I am working on at the moment. I can just go and pick it up where I left off the previous night. There is no washing up to do, no dirty clothes on the floor – that's how I try to arrange things to make it easier to use my time properly. Things are different when one gets into the third age, with two hip replacements and a shoulder operation, and one has to adapt one's time to it.

Since I've been working in an interdisciplinary way – rehearsing with actors rather than working as a designer on my own – we are of course working to time. I don't plan what I want to achieve in a whole day but how many small pieces will fit in. Especially working with top-range actors requires timely starts and finishes, looking at the watch and making effective use of the time we have together – proceed bit by bit, keep up the momentum and achieve what we planned to do in the day. Being a director/creator means being in the driver's seat – and the responsibility goes beyond: the entire team also need to anticipate the next steps, prepare for them without losing time or unnecessary waiting. I have to think in advance and come prepared so that we can focus on the art of making theatre.

In 2009, the artistic director of the Tricycle Theatre in Kilburn in London, Nicolas Kent, proposed a major project. With the literary manager of the National Theatre, they commissioned twelve plays, each of thirty-minute duration, from different writers under the title *The Great Game*. The show would describe the world of Afghanistan from the start of the British occupation to the present day. These plays could be seen either over three evenings at four plays a night or at weekend 'marathons' starting at 10 am and ending at 10 pm. Nick wanted to work with someone who would not conventionally design but could create a framework for the plays and then with simple additions make them specific to each individual play. Their idea was also that the writers would be given no more than a date for their play, and there would be no interference until the submission date from anyone. We, as the creative group, would get them in order of events in Afghanistan and make minor suggestions if necessary. I knew the Tricycle (now called Kiln Theatre) well, having been involved with it since its beginning in 1980, and also knew the Kilburn community, consisting largely of settled Irish, Jewish and Jamaican immigrants, stretching out into the more elegant areas of Hampstead, Maida Vale and Cricklewood. I accepted the invitation and began to wonder how I could begin, never ever believing I could find a solution – once again walking hand in hand with fear. In my studio, I have a large black portfolio labelled 'Ideas & Inspirations'. I do not look at it often, but it is always an arsenal for new thoughts. In it I found a sketch I had made from memory following a flight to Romania, when we could not land for about forty minutes and the plane was circling round a patchwork of dry fields. I looked at the sketch and thought I could make a floor cloth out of different pieces of dyed fireproof hessian fabric pieces, and finding some samples I started making a scale model to fit the Tricycle stage floor – something that could roll up easily for storage or possibly for touring the production, which was under discussion.

By chance, I picked up an old copy of the *New York Times*, and while idly glancing through it came across an obituary of the Afghan painter Ustad Mashal (1917–98) from Herat. He was famous for his skill at painting Persian miniatures, but suddenly felt an impulse to paint a large mural depicting 500 years of Afghanistan on the blank wall of the Bazaar in Herat outside his workroom. He started with the imaginary figure of the Queen of Herat and the image of the young revolutionary girl who defied the British occupation, and sketched in other historic figures. All the time Mashal was working on the mural, he was unaware that he was being watched by members of the Taliban. Suddenly they came in with buckets of whitewash. They threw the whitewash over the mural and pinned him down to the ground and made him watch the destruction of his work. By a miracle, he escaped and got a passage to New York, where he spent the second part of his life. I showed this to the director Nick Kent and offered a solution: *What if – as the audience come in – they see a man painting a mural – maybe up a ladder, maybe with pop music on a radio, when suddenly all the auditorium doors open and men dressed as Taliban come in with buckets of whitewash and the mural becomes a white wall onto which projections could be shown?* – as I knew that one play would be about the destruction of the Twin Towers in New York in 2001. Nick agreed. Of course, our mural had protective sealant, and the stage management simply stayed on after the performance to wash the whitewash off. It was the visual equivalent of starting an opera on a top note – and with these two elements I began to compose the visual Afghan symphony.

Then I read about the American 'Opium War' against Afghanistan where they intended to burn the poppy fields and impose the slogan *Burn the Poppies – Plant Wheat Instead*. As the First World War poppy fields of Flanders show, poppies are indestructible, and even in burnt fields they will grow again. By chance – and in my life, so many things have happened to me 'by chance' – I saw an advert in a local paper for an artificial flower business that was closing down. So, I went to have a look and bought a bunch of pink silk poppies. I saw they were made in Taiwan, where I knew several former students. I contacted them, and a few weeks later 200 pink silk poppies were delivered to the Tricycle Theatre to make the background to the patchwork field of hessian. The mural that initially showed the painting, and was then whitewashed, was in a hydraulic frame. And when a film of the destruction of the Twin Towers was projected on the whitewashed surface, the mural disappeared into the sky revealing a field of poppies against a blue sky. The message was clear. The visual metaphor conveyed the story underlying centuries of Afghan history as well as tyranny, oppression and destruction anywhere in the world.

The Great Game started at the Tricycle Theatre in Kilburn in 2009, and by popular demand came back again in 2010 prior to a tour starting at the Sidney Harman Hall in Washington, DC, where President Barack Obama and his wife attended the performance. Then the show toured to the Guthrie Theatre Minneapolis, to Berkeley

Rep and, finally, to the Public Theatre in New York. After the tour, we returned to the UK exhausted but happy and put everything into store. To our surprise, we were 'commanded' by President Barack Obama to return to the Harman Center for the Arts for two special encore performances offered free to soldiers, wounded veterans and government officials involved in the war in Afghanistan. There was a deep thrill for us all hearing an audience fall silent, rapt in the drama.

On 25 April 2009, Michael Billington wrote of our production appreciatively in *The Guardian*:

> but these plays give us the chance to make an informed judgment. And I can only salute the entire cast, including Ramon Tikaram, Vincent Ebrahim, Daniel Betts and Jemma Redgrave, and the design of Pamela Howard and Miriam Nabarro. Something remarkable is happening at the Tricycle, where Afghan history and culture are being made manifest in a uniquely challenging, theatrically exciting way. (Billington 2009)

In *The Observer*, Susannah Clapp wrote on 26 April 2009:

> At its best, it demonstrates dramatically rather than explaining. Pamela Howard's vivid painted backdrop shows honey-coloured rock, a vestigially monumental Buddha statue and beards floating among clouds. The painting is first Talibanned: denounced and daubed over with whitewash with disconcerting realism. [. . .] Later as the Twin Towers fall, it topples down, giving way to a Technicolor cerulean sky and poppy field. (Clapp 2009)

And that's all I tried to do.

On 8 August 2021, Christina Lamb in her *Sunday Times* report of the worsening situation in Afghanistan quotes the voice of a 34-year-old artist – part of the ArtLords consortium of graffiti artists, looking out of a window and reflecting:

> Our only weapons are brushes and paints but art is more important than ever and we will resist. (Lamb 2021)

As artists making theatre, we have to have our equipment ready and prepared for the next move in order to realise our Arsenal of Dreams. That is our ammunition!

WORKS CITED

Allin, John and Arnold Wesker (1974), *Say Goodbye: You May Never See Them Again*, London: Jonathan Cape.

Backemeyer, Sylvia, ed. (1997), *Ralph Koltai: Designer for the Stage*, London: Lund Humphries.

Billington, Michael (2009), 'The Great Game: Afghanistan', *The Guardian*, 25 April 2009. Available online: https://www.theguardian .com/stage/2009/apr/25/tricycle-theatre-great-game-afghanistan (accessed 6 September 2021).

Brecht, Bertolt (1965), *The Messingkauf Dialogues*, trans. John Willett, London: Methuen.

Clapp, Susannah (2009), 'From Kabul to Kilburn the Hard Way: It's a Brave Venture to Devote a Two-Month Festival to the History of Afghanistan. But Where Are the Country's Own Writers?: The Great Game Tricycle, London NW6, to 14 June', *The Observer*, 26 April 2009, 15. Available online: Gale Academic OneFile: link.gale.com/a pps/doc/A198731973/AONE?u=unihull&sid=bookmark-AONE&xid =56793d02 (accessed 6 September 2021).

Gruhl, Boris Michael (2010), 'Im freien Lauf der Fantasie: Das Janáček Festival in Brno beginnt traumhaft', *nmz online*, 19 November 2010. Available online: https://www.nmz.de/online/im-freien-lauf-der -fantasie-das-janaceks-festival-in-brno-beginnt-traumhaft (accessed 6 September 2021).

Howard, Pamela (2009), *What Is Scenography?* 2nd edn., New York and London: Routledge.

Howard, Pamela (2011), 'Staging *Brouček*: The World Premiere of *Výlet pana Broučka do Měsíce* by Leoš Janáček', in Christian M. Billing and Pavel Drábek (eds), *Czech Stage Art and Stage Design*. Special issue of *Theatralia*, 14 (1): 292–308. Available online: https://digilib.phil.muni .cz/handle/11222.digilib/115558 (accessed 6 September 2021).

Howard, Pamela (2019), *What Is Scenography?* 3rd revised and enlarged edn., ed. Pavel Drábek, New York and London: Routledge.

Krivine, Frédéric at al. (2009), 'The Duty to Remember', Season 6, Episode 5 of *A French Village (Un village français)*. Dir. Thierry Jault. Tétra Média, Terego.

Kustow, Michael (2009), *In Search of Jerusalem*, London: Oberon Books.

Lamb, Christina (2021), 'Orchestras and Artists of Afghanistan Insist Taliban Won't Stop the Music', *The Sunday Times*, 8 August 2021. Available online: https://www.thetimes.co.uk/article/orchestras-and -artists-of-afghanistan-insist-taliban-wont-stop-the-music-8r06jmx00 (accessed 6 September 2021).

Matras, Yaron (2014), *I Met Lucky People: The Story of the Romani Gypsies*, London: Penguin Books.

Mendel, Janet (2002), *My Kitchen in Spain: 225 Authentic Regional Recipes*, New York: HarperCollins.

New King James Version (1982), Nashville: HarperCollins Christian Publishing. Available online: https://www.biblegateway.com/versions/ New-King-James-Version-NKJV-Bible/ (accessed 6 September 2021).

Salomon, Charlotte (1981), *Charlotte: Life or Theater*, New York: The Viking Press.

Shakespeare, William ([c. 1592–3] 2009), *King Richard III*, ed. James R. Siemon, The Arden Shakespeare, London and New York: Bloomsbury.

Shakespeare, William ([c. 1595–6] 2017), *A Midsummer Night's Dream*, ed. Sukanta Chaudhuri, The Arden Shakespeare, London and New York: Bloomsbury.

Wesker, Arnold (2008), *All Things Tire of Themselves*, foreword by Michael Kustow, Hexham: Flambard Press.

.

INDEX